Start Investing in Gold & Silver

Start Investing in Gold & Silver

A modern guide to hedging your money with precious metals

Calen Hart

Mindful Pages

Published in 2025

ISBN: 9789371773584 (PB)
ISBN: 9789371774598 (eBook)

Published by

Mindful Pages
Imprint of Alpha Editions LLC
312 W. 2nd St #1834
Casper, WY 82601, USA

This book was developed using advanced writing tools to support the drafting and ideation process. All content has been thoughtfully curated, refined, and reviewed to ensure quality and relevance.

Content

Introduction
Owning Reality in an Age of Illusion

Money, once a concrete measure of value anchored in gold, silver, or tangible exchange, has gradually become an ethereal construct. In the contemporary financial landscape, wealth often exists less as something you can hold and more as numbers flickering across screens, shaped by algorithms, policy decisions, and the intangible trust we place in institutions. It is a realm where central banks, digital ledgers, and complex derivatives dictate outcomes, rather than physical assets that endure. This transformation prompts a pressing question: in such an abstracted world, what can an individual rely upon when the foundation beneath money feels so insubstantial?

Start Investing in Gold & Silver: A Modern Guide to Hedging Your Money with Precious Metals offers a compelling answer. It urges readers to reconnect with a form of wealth that resists the ephemerality of digital finance—precious metals. Gold and silver, after all, are not merely investment vehicles; they are elemental anchors in a fluid and often unpredictable system. The book does more than outline acquisition strategies; it reawakens a deeply human instinct: the desire for permanence amid uncertainty. To own these metals is, fundamentally, to reclaim a stake in what endures.

The urgency of this perspective cannot be overstated. Over the past century, monetary systems have transformed profoundly. Abandoning the gold standard severed the formal link between currency and tangible assets, ushering in the era of fiat money. Governments and central banks gained unprecedented ability to manipulate currencies, inflate economies, and influence markets—tools that, while stabilising in the short term, create vulnerabilities that surface in moments of crisis. Inflation, devaluation, and financial instability are persistent reminders that wealth preservation demands foresight and prudence. How, then, can individuals protect their capital in a system designed, in subtle ways, to erode it?

Beyond economics lies the psychological dimension. Humans crave substance—not merely for utility, but for trust, symbolism, and reassurance. Across cultures and epochs, gold and silver have embodied these qualities, representing stability, beauty, and permanence. Unlike digital assets or complex financial instruments, these metals are tangible, universally recognised, and largely impervious to the whims of technology or policy. The book delves into why, even in a high-tech era, these intrinsic qualities maintain their resonance—and why recognising this matters for today's investors.

Start Investing in Gold & Silver distinguishes itself by intertwining practical strategy with philosophical reflection. Investing is framed not merely as a transactional act but as a conscious statement about values and foresight. What does it mean to hold something that cannot be conjured by policy, inflated at will, or erased by a digital glitch? How does the tangible presence of precious metals recalibrate one's sense of security, autonomy, and identity? These questions form the backbone of the book's narrative, blending technical guidance with existential inquiry.

The chapters unfold in a layered exploration. Initially, the historical and psychological significance of gold and silver is examined, illustrating why these metals endure while other forms of wealth falter. Practical guidance follows: evaluating market signals, deciding when metals are appropriate, securing and storing them prudently, and balancing physical holdings with contemporary digital tools. Ethical considerations are woven throughout, emphasising the moral clarity that tangible assets can offer in a financial landscape increasingly dominated by opacity and abstraction.

This approach encourages readers to perceive precious metals not as relics but as instruments of resilience. The book challenges the prevailing orthodoxy that digital and paper assets alone suffice, instead proposing a broader, more grounded conception of wealth—one that privileges permanence, trust, and autonomy alongside liquidity and growth.

Confronting the realities of fragile fiat currencies, market volatility, and political risk is uncomfortable, yet it also illuminates opportunity. Investors attuned to systemic signals and psychological undercurrents may find that gold and silver offer both protection and a foundation for enduring security.

Choosing to invest in precious metals extends beyond monetary calculation; it is a deliberate assertion of values. It proclaims that some forms of wealth should remain inviolate, irrespective of economic tides or technological fads. This book aims to guide readers thoughtfully through this terrain, advocating mindful engagement rather than anxious reaction.

As the text unfolds, rigorous analysis sits alongside narrative insight; practical instruction accompanies philosophical reflection. The complexities of the metals market, and the wider financial ecosystem, demand such depth. A surface-level approach is insufficient; one must understand history, human behaviour, and strategic considerations in concert.

In holding gold and silver, readers do more than acquire assets—they reaffirm a connection to permanence, a tangible defence against impermanence and fragility. This book cultivates that understanding, grounding financial decisions in reality even as the surrounding world becomes increasingly abstract and uncertain.

Ultimately, this guide is about more than metals: it is a manifesto for clarity, sovereignty, and enduring value in an era dominated by illusion. It invites readers to reclaim control, anchoring wealth in what is real, enduring, and fundamentally trustworthy.

Chapter 1
What's Real Anymore? Why We Long for the Tangible

The evolution of money from a tangible asset to an abstract promise represents one of the most consequential shifts in modern finance—one whose ramifications ripple far beyond the balance sheets into psychology, culture, and trust itself. For centuries, currencies were anchored in something unmistakably real: gold, silver, and other precious metals whose intrinsic value transcended borders and generations. The gold standard tied money directly to these commodities, constraining governments from creating currency at whim and offering a concrete foundation for economic exchange. Yet, over the twentieth century, that anchor was deliberately severed. The abandonment of gold-backed currencies in favour of fiat money untethered value from any physical reality. Today, what we call wealth often exists only as a collective belief—dependent on trust in central banks, government policies, and digital networks rather than the solidity of something one can physically hold.

This Great Decoupling—the deliberate break between money and metal—carries profound consequences that extend well beyond economic mechanics. It challenges fundamental assumptions about the nature of money and how it should function. While fiat currency introduces flexibility and tools to manage economies, it also exposes systemic vulnerabilities: unchecked inflation, currency devaluation, and the gradual erosion of purchasing power. Detached from tangible assets, money becomes simultaneously omnipresent and elusive; it shapes life in every respect yet slips through one's grasp like smoke. Individuals now confront a paradox: wealth is everywhere, and yet nowhere.

To grasp why this matters, one must consider human nature itself. Behavioural psychology and anthropology consistently demonstrate that people instinctively trust what they can see and touch. Gold and silver, in their permanence and weight, resonate at a deeply primal level, evoking security that no digital asset—however sophisticated—can replicate. These metals are far more than commodities; they are enduring symbols embedded in the human psyche. Their lustre and tangibility provide solace amid financial turbulence, acting as emotional anchors in a world dominated by abstraction. This often-overlooked dimension is essential for understanding the sustained allure of precious metals.

The rise of cryptocurrencies and other digital assets might seem to challenge traditional notions of value, yet their very existence highlights the contrast between ephemeral and enduring wealth. Digital assets promise efficiency, decentralisation, and speed, yet they are intrinsically fragile—vulnerable to hacks, regulatory intervention, or systemic failure. When the networks falter, the "wealth" they represent can vanish in an instant. Gold and silver, by contrast, offer resilience: tangible, universally recognised, and largely impervious to the vagaries of code or policy. They provide a grounding counterpoint to the fragility of entirely digital systems.

History reinforces this perspective. Across millennia, societies have turned to gold and silver as repositories of value, especially during upheaval. Wars, hyperinflation, regime changes, and societal collapse repeatedly demonstrated that these metals preserve wealth where other forms of money fail. Their permanence is not simply anecdotal; it is rooted in the chemical and physical properties of the metals combined with their cultural and social significance. Unlike fiat currency or digital entries, gold and silver cannot be created arbitrarily. Their scarcity and durability confer a unique quality: enduring wealth that transcends governments and economic cycles.

This historical insight is crucial for understanding contemporary finance. Amid rising debt, geopolitical uncertainty, and inflationary pressures, conventional assets tied to fiat systems carry hidden risks. Where once paper money offered assurance, now it offers only conditional trust. Individuals seeking stability increasingly turn to assets that retain intrinsic value, unaffected by policy distortions or market whims. Gold and silver emerge not merely as relics, but as pragmatic instruments for hedging against systemic vulnerabilities.

This chapter explores these themes in depth. It traces the shift from gold-backed currency to fiat money, showing why the detachment from tangible assets matters profoundly today. It then examines the psychological underpinnings of our attachment to substance, explaining why the human mind instinctively gravitates toward what it can hold. From there, the discussion turns to digital assets and the paradox they present: innovation shadowed by fragility. Finally, it surveys the historical record, illustrating how gold and silver have repeatedly acted as bulwarks against economic and political turmoil.

Readers will gain a nuanced understanding not only of money's evolution but also of why precious metals occupy a singular position in both history and human experience. The chapter encourages a reconsideration of what "real" wealth means—moving beyond the abstract and reasserting clarity amid complexity. It provides a foundation for the practical and philosophical insights developed throughout the rest of the book.

Engaging with these ideas requires more than passive reading; it demands critical reflection on value and the forces shaping modern finance. What does it truly mean to own wealth in a world dominated by intangible claims? How does one reconcile the efficiency and convenience of digital finance with the enduring human need for permanence and security? By confronting these questions directly, the chapter primes readers to make informed, confident decisions about incorporating precious metals into their financial lives.

Ultimately, the human yearning for the tangible transcends mere prudence—it reflects a fundamental truth. In a world cluttered with ephemeral promises and flickering digital entries, gold and silver provide steady reassurance. They remind us that real wealth is not merely a number on a screen but something that can be held, stored, and passed to future generations. This chapter illuminates that truth with clarity and rigor, bridging historical insight, psychological understanding, and practical guidance for navigating the complex financial landscape of today.

The Great Decoupling: When Money Lost Its Anchor

Money, at its essence, is a social contract—a shared belief in value that facilitates exchange, stores wealth, and expresses trust within a community. For most of human history, this trust was anchored in the tangible: gold and silver, metals whose rarity and physicality imbued them with enduring worth. The connection was not merely symbolic; it was a practical safeguard. Currency represented a claim on a fixed, physical asset, a limit on arbitrary expansion, and a measure of stability. Yet over the twentieth century, this relationship unraveled in what might be termed *the Great Decoupling*: the deliberate separation of money from any intrinsic physical backing. The shift from gold-backed currencies to fiat systems did more than alter monetary policy; it fundamentally transformed the nature of money itself, detaching it from a reliable, physical anchor and recasting it as an abstract, trust-based instrument. Understanding this transformation—and why it matters today—is essential to grasping both the vulnerabilities and possibilities embedded in our current financial architecture.

To appreciate the gravity of this shift, one must revisit the era when the gold standard held sway. Established in various forms during the nineteenth and early twentieth centuries, the gold standard tied the value of national currencies directly to specific quantities of gold. This meant that for every unit of currency issued, a government or central bank maintained a corresponding reserve of gold. This system constrained inflationary pressures, imposed fiscal discipline, and facilitated international trade by providing a common denominator of value. The stability that gold provided was neither perfect nor static—wars, economic depressions, and political upheavals exposed weaknesses—but its tangible grounding offered a shared point of reference, a reality check on the excesses of monetary policy.

However, the twentieth century saw mounting tensions strain the gold standard's limits. The financial demands of global conflicts, particularly the two World Wars, compelled governments to print money beyond their gold reserves. The economic devastation of the Great Depression further challenged the rigidity of the system. Nations increasingly resorted to capital controls, devaluations, and alternative arrangements to manage their economies, signalling cracks in the standard's integrity. By 1971, the United States, under President Nixon, officially ended the convertibility of the dollar into gold, effectively dissolving the Bretton Woods system and inaugurating the fiat era. From this moment forward, money became a promise without a fixed physical underpinning.

The implications of this decoupling are profound. Without the discipline imposed by gold backing, governments and central banks gained the latitude to create currency with fewer immediate constraints. This flexibility has enabled unprecedented interventions—quantitative easing, stimulus programmes, and monetary policy adjustments—to address economic crises and promote growth. Yet it has also opened the door to inflationary pressures, currency devaluation, and the gradual erosion of purchasing power. The financial crises of recent decades, including the 2008 global recession and the economic shockwaves triggered by the COVID-19 pandemic, illustrate the delicate balance fiat money systems must maintain. When confidence falters, the intangible nature of fiat currencies becomes a vulnerability rather than a strength.

Critically, this decoupling also reshapes the very meaning of money in society. No longer an object with intrinsic value, currency today is a reflection of collective trust in institutions and policies—trust that can be swift to erode. This introduces a dynamic of fragility where economic stability hinges on perceptions and expectations as much as on fundamentals. The rise of digital currencies, financial derivatives, and complex monetary instruments adds layers of abstraction that further distance money from physical reality. While these innovations offer efficiency and accessibility, they also deepen the challenge of understanding and managing risk.

Yet the story of the Great Decoupling is not one of mere loss; it reveals tensions between control and constraint, innovation and tradition. Fiat money systems have undoubtedly provided tools for managing economic cycles in ways the gold standard could not accommodate. By allowing central banks to adjust supply dynamically, they can respond to deflationary shocks, stimulate demand, and pursue social policy goals. However, the absence of a physical anchor requires ever-greater vigilance and transparency to maintain trust. The fundamental question remains: how sustainable is a system built on trust in institutions and policies that may shift with political winds and global pressures?

This question gains urgency against the backdrop of growing economic uncertainty. Inflation, once a controlled risk, has re-emerged as a significant concern in many advanced economies, threatening to undermine real incomes and savings. Fiscal deficits balloon under social and infrastructural demands, while geopolitical tensions strain global cooperation. In such conditions, the detachment of money from physical assets exposes individuals and institutions to risks that are not always fully priced into markets or understood by the public. The erosion of purchasing power, currency fluctuations, and potential loss of confidence in central banks are not abstract threats but immediate challenges for wealth preservation and financial planning.

It is within this context that gold and silver reclaim their relevance—not as nostalgic relics but as *counterweights* to the vulnerabilities inherent in fiat systems. The physicality of these metals provides a boundary against the risks of monetary excess. Their scarcity and tangible presence anchor value in a way that fiat currencies cannot replicate. Unlike paper or digital money, gold and silver cannot be created by policy decree; their supply is limited by nature and mining realities. This scarcity injects discipline and resilience into wealth storage, especially when confidence in fiat currencies wanes.

Moreover, the Great Decoupling invites a reconsideration of what constitutes real wealth. When money becomes an abstract promise, the distinction between *nominal* and *real* value grows critical. Holding assets tied to physical commodities or commodities themselves can protect against the hidden tax of inflation. This is not merely a defensive manoeuvre; it is a strategic recognition of the changing economic environment. Investors who ignore the implications of the decoupling risk exposure to unseen erosions of capital, while those who understand it can harness metals as a stabilising element within diversified portfolios.

The debate surrounding fiat money versus commodity-backed currency is not without nuance. Proponents of fiat argue that the flexibility it affords is indispensable for modern economies. They point to periods when adherence to gold standards exacerbated recessions or prevented effective policy responses. Conversely, critics warn that the absence of a tangible anchor encourages reckless fiscal behaviour and sows the seeds for monetary crises. History offers examples on both sides: the hyperinflation of Weimar Germany and Zimbabwe illustrate the dangers of unrestrained money printing, while the gold standard's rigidity contributed to prolonged economic pain during the Great Depression.

This tension underscores the complex trade-offs that define monetary systems. The Great Decoupling did not simply sever money from metal; it replaced one set of challenges with another, demanding sophisticated frameworks for trust, regulation, and oversight. Yet the very fact that gold and silver continue to command respect and demand—centuries after the gold standard's demise—speaks volumes about their enduring function as anchors in a sea of uncertainty.

Practically, this has led to a resurgence of interest in precious metals among individuals and institutions seeking refuge from the volatility of fiat currencies. Central banks around the world, once net sellers of gold, have become net buyers in recent decades, signalling a shift in policy and perception. Private investors increasingly allocate portions of their portfolios to physical metals or related instruments. This trend reflects a growing recognition that in a world where money's value is no longer tied to a physical asset, possessing something real and finite offers unique strategic advantages.

The Great Decoupling also has profound implications for the future trajectory of money. Emerging technologies—such as central bank digital currencies (CBDCs) and cryptocurrencies—promise to reshape financial systems again, blending digital innovation with questions about trust and value. However, these developments do not negate the lessons of the past. Rather, they highlight the ongoing need to balance flexibility with stability, abstraction with tangibility. As financial instruments grow more complex, the fundamental question of what constitutes *real* money becomes even more pressing.

In this light, the Great Decoupling is best understood not as a one-time event but as a continuing process—one that challenges us to reconsider the foundations of wealth and value in a rapidly evolving world. Its legacy compels investors, policymakers, and citizens alike to engage with money not as a passive medium but as a dynamic, contested construct. Recognising the loss of money's physical anchor is the first step toward crafting strategies that acknowledge both the promises and perils of modern finance.

Ultimately, the separation of money from gold and silver exposes the fragile architecture upon which contemporary economies rest. It demands a heightened awareness of the forces at play and an active choice about how to preserve and grow wealth. For those willing to grapple with the complexities of this decoupling, precious metals offer not only protection but a reaffirmation of *real* value—an enduring tether to the material world in a time when so much else has become intangible.

The Psychology of Substance: Why We Trust What We Can Hold

The enduring appeal of gold and silver transcends the realm of economics; it is rooted deeply in human psychology and culture. While many modern investors might focus narrowly on market trends, price charts, or geopolitical events, the emotional resonance of precious metals offers a profound, often overlooked dimension of value. Why, in a world awash with digital currencies, complex derivatives, and intangible assets, do gold and silver continue to evoke an almost instinctive trust? This question probes the intersection of behavioural psychology, anthropology, and history—disciplines that reveal precious metals not merely as financial instruments but as *emotional safe havens*. Understanding this psychological substrate is crucial for anyone seeking to appreciate the full significance of metals as part of a resilient wealth strategy.

Humans are fundamentally embodied creatures. Our cognition, decision-making, and sense of security are anchored in physical experience. From infancy, tactile interaction shapes perception and trust: objects we can see, touch, and manipulate register as more 'real' and reliable than abstractions. This grounding in the tangible underpins why precious metals, which possess a distinct sensory presence—weight, texture, and lustre—confer an innate sense of authenticity. Neuroscientific studies of decision-making have demonstrated that physical possession activates different neural pathways than digital or symbolic representations, often invoking feelings of control and permanence. In essence, *the physicality of gold and silver communicates trust on a subconscious level*, bypassing the often volatile rationalisations that govern financial markets.

Anthropological evidence reinforces this psychological insight. Across cultures and epochs, societies have consistently invested precious metals with layers of meaning beyond their material utility. Gold, with its radiant colour and resistance to tarnish, has been emblematic of purity, divinity, and immortality. Silver, often more accessible yet equally lustrous, has symbolised connection, protection, and communal trust. These symbolic dimensions are not mere superstition but reflect a collective, deeply embedded cultural architecture that sustains faith in metals as stable stores of value. This cultural continuity across millennia underscores a social contract with substance—a tacit agreement that gold and silver represent enduring worth precisely because they *are* tangible, universal, and irreplaceable.

The psychology of substance also intersects with risk perception and emotional resilience. Precious metals serve as psychological anchors in times of uncertainty and crisis, offering a sense of security that purely digital or paper assets cannot replicate. Behavioral finance research shows that in moments of market turmoil, investors gravitate toward assets that provide *not only* financial protection but also emotional reassurance. The tactile assurance of holding physical gold or silver can mitigate anxiety and reinforce confidence, functioning as a buffer against the disorienting abstractions of modern finance. This explains the phenomenon of metals often outperforming during periods of geopolitical instability or economic upheaval: their value lies as much in what they *feel* like as in what they *are* worth.

Yet this emotional safety is neither irrational nor naïve; it is an adaptive response to the complexities of trust in contemporary monetary systems. Fiat currencies, digital balances, and electronic payments depend on layers of institutional and technological trust—trust that is inherently fragile and subject to erosion. When headlines report on sovereign debt crises, cyber-attacks, or central bank interventions, the intangibility of modern money can seem precarious. By contrast, gold and silver provide a tangible hedge—a form of wealth that does not depend on third-party assurances, complex networks, or digital infrastructures. This *sovereign quality* of metals resonates deeply with individuals seeking autonomy and control over their financial destiny.

Critically, this psychological dimension coexists with—and enhances—the economic utility of precious metals. While metals do carry intrinsic and industrial value, it is their role as *universal symbols of trust* that amplifies their function as stores of value. This duality explains why metals retain liquidity and purchasing power even when other assets falter. For instance, during the hyperinflation episodes of the twentieth century—from Weimar Germany to Zimbabwe—gold and silver preserved wealth when currencies became worthless. Their physical substance rendered them immune to the arbitrary destruction of value that paper money suffers under inflationary regimes. This historical precedent aligns with contemporary investor behaviour, illustrating that trust in the physical endures as a fundamental hedge against systemic risk.

The intersection of cultural anthropology and behavioural psychology also sheds light on the enduring ritualistic and social functions of precious metals. Coins and bullion are not simply transactional objects; they carry narratives of lineage, legacy, and identity. Gifting a gold wedding band, for example, conveys trust and permanence far beyond the material. Collectors and investors often describe their holdings with affection and respect, framing metals as personal guardians of wealth and history. These narratives enrich the relationship between holder and metal, fostering a psychological bond that digital assets struggle to replicate. This bond encourages stewardship, patience, and a long-term perspective—qualities that are invaluable in navigating volatile markets.

However, it is important to acknowledge contrasting perspectives that question the psychological premium accorded to precious metals. Critics argue that emotional attachment can cloud rational investment decisions, leading to overconcentration or neglect of portfolio diversification. Furthermore, the physical possession of metals entails logistical challenges—storage, security, and liquidity concerns—that digital assets ostensibly circumvent. These critiques merit consideration; yet they often underestimate the *integrative role* that psychological security plays within a comprehensive wealth strategy. Rather than viewing emotional attachment as a liability, it can be understood as a crucial component of risk management—one that addresses not only market risks but also human behavioural realities.

Modern applications of this insight are evident in the growing interest in tangible asset classes amid rising economic uncertainties. Wealth advisors increasingly recognise that portfolios which incorporate physical metals can better accommodate investor psychology, providing a stabilising counterbalance to volatile digital and paper assets. The popularity of gold-backed exchange-traded funds (ETFs) and bullion products reflects a desire to capture both the emotional and financial benefits of metals without sacrificing convenience. Yet even these innovations ultimately depend on the underlying physical substance to maintain trust. The metal's tangibility remains the final arbiter of value, distinguishing it from purely synthetic financial instruments.

At a broader societal level, the psychology of substance invites reflection on the meaning of money itself. It challenges prevailing notions that wealth is solely a matter of numerical accumulation or digital entries, reasserting the importance of *embodiment* and *permanence*. In a financial landscape characterised by rapid change, innovation, and sometimes opacity, precious metals provide an anchor not just for portfolios but for human confidence in the very concept of value. This relationship between trust and tangibility is not static; it evolves with cultural shifts and technological developments. Yet, as history and psychology attest, the fundamental human craving for substance endures.

Engaging with this psychological dimension enriches the conversation around investing in gold and silver, transforming it from a mere calculation of returns to a more holistic understanding of what it means to hold and trust wealth. It reveals precious metals as complex, multi-layered assets that satisfy both the mind and the heart, the intellect and the instincts. For those navigating the uncertainties of modern finance, recognising the deep roots of this trust offers clarity and confidence—a reminder that in a world increasingly shaped by the intangible, the tangible remains a source of profound reassurance.

Digital Riches, Fragile Fortunes

In a world captivated by the promise of digital innovation, few developments have sparked as much fascination—and controversy—as cryptocurrencies and digital assets. Their rapid ascent has been heralded as a revolutionary shift in how value is created, stored, and transferred. Yet beneath the dazzling headlines and speculative fervour lies a more nuanced reality: digital wealth, while offering unparalleled convenience and accessibility, carries vulnerabilities that sharply contrast with the enduring solidity of precious metals. This contrast is not a battle of antagonists but a revealing juxtaposition that forces us to confront fundamental questions about trust, permanence, and resilience in an increasingly virtual financial landscape. Most pressing among these is: what happens when the cloud collapses?

The appeal of cryptocurrencies like Bitcoin, Ethereum, and myriad altcoins rests on their promise to decentralise finance, bypass traditional institutions, and create a transparent, immutable ledger of transactions. At first glance, these innovations appear to embody the future of money—a digital native form, untethered from physical constraints and resistant to censorship. The blockchain technology underlying many cryptocurrencies offers remarkable features: decentralisation, cryptographic security, and programmability. For users seeking freedom from centralised control or inflationary fiat regimes, digital assets can appear as a potent antidote. However, it is precisely these characteristics that expose their fragility.

Unlike physical gold or silver, digital assets exist entirely within electronic networks—complex webs of servers, nodes, and protocols that are susceptible to failure. While blockchain technology is designed to be resilient, no system is immune to risks inherent in its infrastructure. Cybersecurity threats loom large: exchanges and wallets have been hacked, private keys lost or stolen, and vulnerabilities exploited to devastating effect. In 2014, Mt. Gox, once the largest Bitcoin exchange, collapsed under the weight of fraud and mismanagement, wiping out hundreds of millions of dollars of user assets. More recently, decentralized finance (DeFi) platforms, despite their promise of trustless transactions, have been plagued by smart contract bugs and exit scams, undermining confidence. These incidents underscore a critical truth: digital riches are only as secure as the weakest link in an intricate technological chain.

Beyond technical vulnerabilities, digital assets face regulatory uncertainties that compound their fragility. Governments worldwide are grappling with how to integrate cryptocurrencies into existing legal frameworks. Actions range from outright bans to cautious acceptance and experimentation with central bank digital currencies (CBDCs). Regulatory shifts can dramatically affect asset valuations and user access. For example, China's repeated clampdowns on crypto mining and trading in recent years caused significant market disruptions. This dependency on evolving political landscapes introduces an element of unpredictability absent from physical metals, which are immune to policy whims in their fundamental nature.

Moreover, digital assets depend on the continuous availability of electricity, internet connectivity, and functioning hardware. These dependencies raise existential questions about long-term storage and survivability under extreme conditions. While proponents emphasise blockchain's decentralised resilience, the reality is that access to one's digital wealth hinges on maintaining functional devices, secure passwords, and active platforms. Forgotten private keys or obsolete wallets can render assets irretrievable, as countless anecdotal stories attest. The contrast with physical metals is stark: a gold coin requires no password, no network, no software update. It is tangible, verifiable, and unyielding to the vulnerabilities of cyberspace.

This dependence on infrastructure provokes the compelling thought experiment posed by the notion of a "cloud collapse"—a sudden failure or degradation of digital systems, whether due to cyberattack, natural disaster, or systemic technological breakdown. In such a scenario, digital wealth risks becoming inaccessible or devalued overnight. Although such events are often dismissed as improbable, history offers sobering reminders that technology-dependent systems are vulnerable to cascading failures. The 2008 global financial crisis, while rooted in traditional finance, revealed how interconnections can amplify shocks. Similarly, cyber warfare and critical infrastructure attacks are increasingly recognised as real threats to economic stability. In contrast, gold and silver—stored securely and physically separate from digital networks—maintain intrinsic value regardless of the state of technology.

The contrasting qualities of digital and physical assets invite a deeper reflection on the nature of trust. Digital currencies rely on cryptographic proofs and consensus algorithms, shifting trust from institutions to code. This *trustless* architecture is revolutionary but abstract, mediated by layers of technical complexity that remain opaque to many users. Physical metals, conversely, require trust in tangible reality: the human senses, metallurgy, and centuries of cultural consensus. While neither form of trust is absolute or immune to failure, the psychological comfort derived from physical substance cannot be discounted. It addresses a fundamental human need for certainty in an uncertain world.

Yet digital assets should not be dismissed outright as fragile illusions. They represent a significant evolution in financial technology with genuine utility and potential for disruption. Their agility, divisibility, and programmability enable novel applications—from smart contracts to cross-border payments—that physical metals cannot match. For many investors, cryptocurrencies form a dynamic component of diversified portfolios, offering exposure to innovation alongside traditional assets. The tension lies in recognising that digital and physical wealth serve complementary functions rather than mutually exclusive roles.

Practical strategies increasingly reflect this duality. Hybrid approaches blend physical gold and silver with digital holdings, leveraging the strengths of each while mitigating their respective weaknesses. Such balance acknowledges the convenience and growth potential of digital assets alongside the enduring security of metals. The challenge for investors is to understand the distinct risk profiles and to resist the temptation to conflate convenience with resilience. Digital riches may promise speed and innovation, but fragile fortunes are built when physical anchors are absent.

This discussion also highlights ethical and philosophical dimensions. Digital currencies are often praised for their democratizing potential—empowering individuals excluded from traditional banking, promoting financial sovereignty, and fostering transparency. However, the environmental costs of energy-intensive mining and the volatility that fuels speculative excesses raise critical questions about sustainability and responsibility. Physical metals, while not without environmental and geopolitical concerns, embody a form of wealth preservation that transcends cycles of innovation and obsolescence. Their permanence challenges us to consider what value truly endures beyond the shifting sands of technology.

Ultimately, the juxtaposition of digital assets and precious metals compels a reassessment of modern wealth paradigms. It urges investors to look beyond hype and novelty, to consider foundational principles of security, trust, and tangibility. What survives the collapse of digital infrastructures is not a question of technological inevitability but one of preparedness and perspective. In navigating this complex terrain, the wisdom of holding physical metals alongside digital riches emerges as a prudent strategy—not a rejection of progress, but a sober acknowledgment of human and systemic limitations.

As the financial landscape continues to evolve, the dialogue between digital innovation and elemental substance will shape the contours of investment philosophy. Understanding the fragility inherent in digital wealth—and the irreplaceable security offered by physical metals—equips investors to make informed choices that withstand not only market cycles but the deeper uncertainties of our interconnected world.

The Timelessness Test: What Survives Across Centuries?

Throughout history, the true measure of any store of value has been its capacity to endure. In a world marked by war, economic upheaval, regime changes, and systemic collapse, few assets have demonstrated the resilience and reliability that precious metals—specifically gold and silver—have consistently exhibited. Far from being antiquated relics or mere symbols of bygone eras, these metals have proven themselves as survivors, bearing witness to human civilisation's most tumultuous moments and preserving wealth where all else has faltered. Examining how various societies have turned to gold and silver in times of crisis offers crucial insight into their unique role—not only as monetary instruments but as bulwarks of permanence amid impermanence.

The story begins with the recognition that economic and political systems, no matter how advanced or complex, are inherently fragile. Currency regimes have collapsed, empires have fallen, and financial systems have been reset countless times throughout history. Paper money, fiat currencies, and even digital balances exist as fragile social contracts that can be broken or rendered meaningless when trust erodes or governments disintegrate. In contrast, precious metals maintain value independent of any particular state or institution. Their worth derives from physical properties—scarcity, divisibility, durability—and from a shared human consensus that transcends time and place. This universal acceptance has enabled gold and silver to function as *portable wealth* that can be stored, hidden, or transported across borders, preserving purchasing power when paper or digital money cannot.

Consider one of history's most instructive examples: the fall of the Roman Empire. As Rome's political and economic structures crumbled in the fifth century AD, the value of Roman currency rapidly deteriorated amid rampant inflation and political chaos. Yet archaeological discoveries reveal that gold and silver coins remained a reliable medium of exchange and store of value throughout this period. Wealthy individuals and merchants often converted their assets into bullion or coinage, effectively shielding themselves from the devaluation that afflicted the official currency. This pattern repeated itself through various eras—from the Byzantine Empire's coinage resilience during sieges to the use of silver as a hedge during China's dynastic upheavals.

The experience of hyperinflation provides another powerful testament to the timelessness of metals. The hyperinflation in Weimar Germany during the early 1920s, often cited as a cautionary tale, rendered the Papiermark worthless overnight. Ordinary citizens witnessed their savings evaporate as prices soared exponentially. In stark contrast, those who held gold retained purchasing power. Indeed, gold's role as a safeguard during periods of extreme inflation has been well documented worldwide, including in Latin America during the late twentieth century and Zimbabwe in the 2000s. This historical evidence underscores a fundamental economic truth: while fiat currencies are vulnerable to policy-induced erosion, gold and silver represent a fixed supply that cannot be inflated into oblivion.

Regime change and political instability also illustrate the strategic utility of precious metals. During revolutions, civil wars, or authoritarian takeovers, official currencies often lose legitimacy, become subject to confiscation, or cease to function effectively in daily commerce. Yet gold and silver, by virtue of their intrinsic and widely recognised value, provide continuity and liquidity. For instance, during the Cuban Revolution and subsequent economic sanctions, many Cubans resorted to gold as a means of preserving wealth and facilitating trade beyond official channels. Similarly, during the collapse of the Soviet Union, precious metals helped bridge the transition from a centrally planned economy to market mechanisms. In these cases, metals offered a form of *economic sovereignty* amid political upheaval, empowering individuals to navigate uncertainty with a tangible asset in hand.

Even in more recent financial crises, the narrative holds. The 2008 global financial crisis triggered widespread loss of confidence in banks and financial instruments. Central banks responded with expansive monetary easing, leading to concerns about currency debasement. Investors flocked to gold, pushing prices to multi-year highs as a hedge against systemic risk. This modern example echoes the lessons of the past: when conventional financial systems falter, metals remain a trusted refuge.

Critically, this enduring value is not solely a function of scarcity or physical attributes but also a reflection of *cultural continuity and collective memory*. Human societies have long imbued gold and silver with symbolic significance—associations with power, purity, and trust—that reinforce their economic role. This cultural resonance amplifies metals' appeal as stores of value, imbuing them with a psychological dimension that survives beyond market fluctuations or policy changes. Unlike ephemeral financial instruments, metals carry a narrative of permanence that appeals to deeply rooted instincts for security and legacy.

Sceptics might argue that precious metals lack yield, are subject to theft or loss, and can be volatile in the short term. While these points warrant consideration, they overlook the broader function metals serve as *foundational wealth anchors*. Metals are not primarily vehicles for rapid growth; rather, they provide a stable base from which investors can weather crises and preserve capital. Their capacity to maintain purchasing power across centuries, through circumstances that have obliterated other assets, remains unmatched.

This longevity is further evidenced by metals' role in legacy planning and intergenerational wealth transfer. Families and institutions have relied on gold and silver to transmit wealth through uncertain times, ensuring that value endures beyond immediate market conditions. The physical nature of metals—durable, portable, universally recognised—makes them uniquely suited to this purpose. Their timelessness is a practical tool for safeguarding not just wealth but *options* for future generations.

The implications for contemporary investors are clear. While modern portfolios often emphasise diversification among equities, bonds, and digital assets, the historical record insists on the inclusion of precious metals as *a distinct and irreplaceable class*. Their survival through wars, hyperinflation, regime changes, and systemic collapses offers a hedge that complements, rather than competes with, other assets. Recognising gold and silver as survivors rather than relics reframes their role: they are not nostalgic indulgences but strategic necessities grounded in empirical reality.

Ultimately, the test of time has affirmed what many contemporary trends overlook: value that is tied to physical substance and collective human trust endures beyond the volatility of markets and politics. Gold and silver have traversed the epochs not merely as decorative artefacts but as practical tools of wealth preservation and resilience. Their timelessness challenges us to rethink the foundations of wealth and to embrace assets that offer stability in a world defined by change.

Chapter 2
Gold & Silver as Human Inventions—and Instincts

Gold and silver occupy a singular place in human history—not merely as commodities, but as vessels of deep cultural significance and instinctual value. They are far more than inert elements extracted from the earth; over millennia, they have been woven into myths, rituals, and social codes that shape both collective identity and individual perception. To understand their enduring appeal, one must move beyond market prices and transactional utility, and examine the intricate interplay of symbolism, ethics, and material reality that elevates these metals to a plane both tangible and transcendent. This chapter invites readers to consider gold and silver not merely as geological products, but as human constructs, forged through collective imagination and psychological instinct.

Gold's value is as much cultural as it is economic. Its radiant hue, rarity, and resistance to tarnish have long inspired awe, turning it into a symbol of the divine and the eternal. Across civilizations, gold has been inseparable from power and ritual—from the gilded regalia of ancient Egyptian pharaohs to the wedding bands exchanged in contemporary ceremonies. Its symbolic weight is no accident; humans have historically endowed certain materials with sacred significance to stabilise social hierarchies and anchor personal meaning. This cultural gravitas has underpinned gold's monetary function, reinforcing confidence in its value through shared narratives. Investing in gold, therefore, is simultaneously a financial and a cultural engagement, participating in a lineage of meaning-making that stretches back millennia.

Silver offers a compelling counterpoint. While often overshadowed by gold's grandeur, silver carries a practical and democratic heritage. From Roman denarii to frontier-era silver dollars, it has served as the currency of everyday life, accessible to many and embedded in commerce. Its abundance and lower unit value enabled fluid transactions and broader participation, reinforcing its role as a medium of exchange and a store of value within social systems. Far from being inferior, silver complements gold, demonstrating how accessibility, utility, and communal trust shape a metal's significance alongside aesthetic and symbolic considerations.

Beyond history and culture, gold and silver embody a distinctive ethical and philosophical dimension. In a financial environment rife with complex derivatives, speculative excess, and debt expansion, these metals represent pure, unencumbered value. Their worth does not depend on counterparty solvency, contractual promises, or financial engineering. Owning gold or silver becomes a moral as well as a financial choice—an assertion of clarity and integrity in a landscape often clouded by opacity and systemic risk. This alignment with transparency and permanence resonates with investors seeking security amid contemporary economic uncertainty.

Psychologically, gold and silver satisfy a profound human need for indestructibility. Unlike digital files vulnerable to hacking or deletion, or paper contracts subject to legal challenge, these metals endure physically and chemically. Their permanence provides emotional assurance that transcends numerical valuations, anchoring wealth not only in the present but across generations. This enduring quality makes them uniquely suited for long-term preservation, legacy planning, and protection against systemic shocks that might render other assets illiquid or valueless.

Understanding gold and silver as human creations, shaped by culture and instinct, reframes their role in modern investing. They are not inert relics clinging to past prestige; their value is continuously renewed through collective belief and functional relevance. This chapter examines the layers of meaning embedded in these metals: the mythic resonance of gold, the practical inclusivity of silver, and the ethical clarity both provide in turbulent financial times.

Engaging with these dimensions equips readers to approach precious metals with a holistic perspective—one that transcends price speculation and situates them within enduring frameworks of trust, identity, and permanence. In doing so, it lays the groundwork for practical investment insights, grounded not only in markets but in the human impulses and cultural forces that have sustained gold and silver as pillars of wealth across centuries.

Metal as Myth: How We Made Gold Sacred

Few materials in human history command as much fascination and reverence as gold. Its lustrous sheen, incorruptible nature, and striking rarity have elevated it far beyond mere metal into the domain of myth and meaning. Gold's value has always extended well beyond economics; it is a cultural artefact shaped by centuries of symbolism, ritual, and power. To understand why gold holds such an enduring place in human societies, one must explore how it became sacred—woven into narratives of gods, kings, weddings, and wars that collectively forged its unique status. This exploration reveals that gold's worth is as much a product of human imagination and social structures as it is of its physical properties.

From the earliest known civilizations, gold was treated as divine. Ancient Egyptians revered gold as the flesh of the gods, a metal that embodied immortality and purity. The burial masks of pharaohs, most famously that of Tutankhamun, crafted from solid gold, were not merely displays of wealth but expressions of spiritual significance, linking rulers to deities and the afterlife. This sanctification of gold forged an inseparable connection between the metal and the concept of eternal life—a connection that shaped religious, political, and social hierarchies. The symbolism extended beyond Egypt; the Incas called gold "sweat of the sun," reflecting a universal tendency to associate the metal with celestial forces and supernatural power.

Gold's sacredness found practical expression in the political realm through its association with kingship and sovereignty. Monarchs throughout history adorned themselves with gold crowns, sceptres, and jewellery as tangible markers of divine right and authority. The metal's permanence and resistance to tarnish made it a fitting symbol of unchallengeable power and legitimacy. In medieval Europe, the possession and display of gold were intertwined with political status and governance, reinforcing social stratification and centralised control. Gold's role as a medium of wealth and a marker of prestige cemented its function not only as currency but as an instrument of political theatre and statecraft.

The cultural significance of gold also permeates human rituals of union and commitment. The gold wedding band, for example, embodies centuries of symbolic meaning. Its circular form, representing eternity, combined with gold's enduring qualities, creates a powerful emblem of lifelong fidelity and value. This tradition, originating in ancient Rome and evolving through Christian symbolism, elevates gold from a material commodity to a vessel of personal and social covenant. The ritual use of gold in weddings, religious ceremonies, and rites of passage demonstrates how its sacred aura informs the very fabric of interpersonal and communal relationships.

War and conquest have further shaped gold's mythic stature. Beyond its utilitarian role in financing armies, gold has been a prize and a symbol of victory. Empires expanded not only to gain territory but to acquire gold—the ultimate trophy of power. The Spanish conquest of the Americas was driven in no small part by the lust for gold, a metal that promised both immense wealth and divine favour. This association of gold with triumph and dominance reinforced its mystique, intertwining economic incentives with ideological narratives of superiority and destiny. Yet, this history also exposes gold's darker dimensions—its role in colonial exploitation, conflict, and inequality—adding complexity to its cultural symbolism.

Contrasting perspectives deepen the understanding of gold's sacredness. While many societies have enshrined gold as an object of veneration, others have critiqued or challenged its primacy. Philosophers and religious traditions have at times condemned the obsession with gold as a source of greed and corruption. The tension between gold's symbolic purity and its association with human vice reflects the ambivalence that accompanies all powerful symbols. This dialectic invites reflection on how cultural meanings evolve and how gold's sacrality coexists with ethical considerations about wealth and morality.

In modern contexts, gold's symbolic power persists even as its economic functions evolve. Central banks hold vast gold reserves not solely for financial reasons but as a signal of stability and trustworthiness. Investors view gold as a safe haven, its cultural cachet amplifying its appeal during times of uncertainty. Luxury goods and jewellery continue to leverage gold's aura of exclusivity and permanence. These contemporary manifestations echo ancient themes, demonstrating how the mythic dimensions of gold remain deeply embedded in collective consciousness.

Understanding gold as a cultural invention shaped by myth and ritual enriches the contemporary discourse on investing and wealth preservation. It challenges reductive views that treat gold as merely a commodity or speculative asset. Instead, it situates gold within a broader human context—one where value is constructed through layers of meaning, tradition, and psychological resonance. This perspective illuminates why gold commands such loyalty and respect, even in a world increasingly dominated by intangible financial instruments.

Engaging with the mythology of gold equips readers to approach the metal not just as an investment but as a phenomenon that intersects with identity, power, and human aspiration. It invites a deeper appreciation of why, despite technological and economic revolutions, gold's sacredness endures—a testament to the complex interplay between matter and meaning, history and humanity.

Silver's Hidden Story: The People's Precious Metal

Silver's place in the annals of monetary history is one of quiet yet profound influence—a narrative often overshadowed by the grandeur of gold but no less pivotal in shaping economies and societies. Unlike gold, which has long been associated with kings, gods, and ceremonial splendour, silver has earned its reputation as *the people's precious metal*, a currency of the many rather than the few. Its democratic identity, forged through centuries of widespread use in coinage and commerce, positions silver as both a complement to and a contrast against gold, revealing a multifaceted role that has underpinned economic systems across cultures and epochs.

From the Roman denarius to modern bullion, silver has consistently served as a medium of exchange accessible to ordinary people. In ancient Rome, silver coinage facilitated daily transactions in bustling markets, allowing trade to flourish beyond the elite strata of society. The denarius became the backbone of Roman economic life, supporting military logistics, civic payments, and consumer exchange alike. This wide circulation of silver coins illustrates its essential function as a *democratising force* in monetary systems—enabling participation in economic activity at multiple levels and helping to integrate vast populations under a common currency.

Silver's relative abundance compared to gold underpinned this accessibility. While gold's scarcity rendered it a store of great wealth and prestige, silver's more plentiful supply allowed for smaller denominations, greater liquidity, and flexibility in everyday trade. This practical utility positioned silver as an indispensable complement to gold, filling the transactional gaps that gold alone could not. Its role as a 'working metal' of commerce facilitated market expansion and economic development, a role that often receives less attention amid gold's symbolic dominance.

The medieval and early modern periods further entrenched silver's status as the currency of the populace. Across Europe, the widespread minting of silver coins enabled burgeoning urban centres and expanding trade networks. The Spanish silver dollar, or "piece of eight," emerged as a global currency during the colonial era, facilitating commerce across continents and oceans. This global circulation of silver coins underscored its function as a unifying medium of exchange, transcending linguistic, cultural, and political boundaries. It also made silver a key instrument in the rise of global capitalism, connecting distant markets in a shared monetary language.

Yet silver's role was not confined to commerce alone; it intersected with social and political structures in complex ways. The democratizing effect of silver coinage challenged existing hierarchies by empowering broader segments of society with economic agency. Access to silver money allowed peasants, artisans, and merchants to participate more fully in economic life, fostering a degree of financial inclusion often lacking in gold-based systems. This historical reality complicates simplistic narratives that privilege gold as the ultimate symbol of wealth, highlighting silver's essential function in everyday economic empowerment.

Silver's democratic identity also manifests in its modern resurgence among investors and collectors. While gold often captures headlines as a haven asset, silver appeals to those seeking a more accessible entry point into precious metals. Its lower price point allows smaller investors to accumulate tangible wealth without prohibitive capital, echoing its historical role as a metal for the many rather than the few. Moreover, silver's industrial applications—ranging from electronics to renewable energy—add layers of practical demand that differentiate it from gold's primarily monetary and ornamental functions. This dual character reinforces silver's status as a versatile asset, blending financial, industrial, and cultural value.

The contrast between gold and silver extends beyond economics into cultural symbolism. Gold's association with divinity, permanence, and exclusivity stands in tension with silver's connotations of utility, adaptability, and inclusiveness. Silver's reflective quality and cooler hue have inspired different mythologies and artistic uses, often linked to the moon and feminine archetypes, as opposed to gold's solar and masculine symbolism. These distinctions enrich the narrative of precious metals, illustrating how cultural meanings shape—and are shaped by—the materials themselves.

Critically, silver's history also highlights the challenges of monetary policy and economic stability. The fluctuation in silver's value, influenced by mining outputs, technological shifts, and monetary reforms, has at times introduced volatility into economies reliant on silver coinage. Debates over bimetallism in the nineteenth century, for example, centred on the relative roles of gold and silver as monetary standards, reflecting tensions between economic inclusion and stability. These historical debates underscore the complex balancing act involved in integrating silver's democratic appeal with broader fiscal policy objectives.

Silver's continued relevance today is visible in both market dynamics and cultural practices. Investors often regard silver as a strategic addition to diversified portfolios, recognising its dual role as a precious metal and an industrial commodity. Its price movements frequently correlate with broader economic indicators, including inflation and industrial demand, making it a unique asset that bridges monetary and practical domains. Collectors and artisans continue to value silver for its aesthetic qualities, maintaining its cultural significance alongside economic utility.

Engaging with silver's hidden story enriches the understanding of precious metals beyond the conventional gold-centric lens. It reveals a metal whose identity is intertwined with the empowerment of ordinary people, economic accessibility, and multifaceted value. This perspective invites a more nuanced appreciation of how silver complements and contrasts with gold, challenging assumptions and expanding the dialogue about what constitutes wealth and value.

For investors and scholars alike, silver's narrative offers practical insights into the dynamics of precious metals markets and the socio-economic forces that shape them. It encourages a holistic view that recognises silver as not merely a lesser counterpart to gold but as a vital, distinct pillar in the architecture of enduring wealth. Understanding silver as *the people's precious metal* provides a foundation for informed decision-making and deeper reflection on the cultural and economic dimensions of metal-based investment.

The Moral Metal: Why We Crave "Clean" Value

In a financial landscape saturated with complexity, obscurity, and frequently unsettling volatility, the appeal of gold and silver extends beyond their economic functions to touch on a deeper, more ethical dimension of value. Amid mounting global debt, rampant financial speculation, and repeated scandals of fraud and manipulation, precious metals emerge not only as tangible assets but as symbols of *"clean" value*—a form of wealth untainted by the moral ambiguities and systemic risks that pervade modern finance. This subchapter explores why investing in metals transcends mere portfolio diversification to become, in many respects, a philosophical act—an assertion of integrity and permanence in a world increasingly defined by ephemeral promises and conditional claims.

The modern monetary system is, at its core, an intricate web of credit and trust, heavily reliant on debt issuance and institutional faith. Sovereign debt levels in major economies now exceed multiples of their gross domestic product, while consumer and corporate indebtedness have soared to unprecedented heights. This expansion of credit, while facilitating economic growth, carries inherent vulnerabilities. When debt balloons beyond sustainable levels, the risk of default, inflationary erosion, and financial crises escalates. These systemic pressures expose the fragility of *paper wealth*—assets whose nominal values depend on complex, often opaque relationships between borrowers, lenders, and regulatory bodies. Against this backdrop, precious metals offer a form of value that is not contingent on counterparty solvency, central bank policies, or political will.

The distinction between "clean" and "dirty" value becomes particularly salient when contrasted with the practices of speculative finance. Derivatives markets, high-frequency trading, and securitised instruments have transformed modern investing into a domain where layers of abstraction often obscure the underlying economic reality. The 2008 global financial crisis starkly illustrated how these abstractions can propagate systemic risk and ethical failure—collapsing trust in institutions and eroding personal wealth. In contrast, gold and silver retain a straightforward, *unambiguous value*, grounded in physical substance and centuries of collective acceptance. Their worth cannot be fabricated, inflated, or engineered through complex financial constructs. This *purity of value* appeals to investors who seek refuge from the opacity and volatility of synthetic assets.

Yet the ethical allure of precious metals extends beyond their tangible nature to encompass broader philosophical concerns about the nature of money and wealth. Investing in gold or silver can be understood as a deliberate stance—a refusal to participate fully in a financial system that, for all its efficiencies, is riddled with moral hazard, speculative excess, and short-termism. It is an embrace of *financial integrity*, prioritising assets whose value is not only transparent but also resistant to manipulation. This stance challenges the prevalent assumption that wealth must be maximised through ever-riskier financial innovation. Instead, it proposes a measured, principled approach that honours stability, transparency, and durability.

Historical episodes reinforce the moral dimension of metals as a refuge from financial turmoil and institutional failure. During periods of hyperinflation, political upheaval, and currency debasement, gold and silver have preserved wealth in ways that paper money could not. For example, during the Weimar Republic's hyperinflation in the early 1920s, citizens who converted their marks into gold retained purchasing power while cash rapidly became worthless. This preservation of value was not simply financial; it was an act of resistance against economic injustice and arbitrary monetary policy. Similarly, in post-Soviet economies, precious metals offered a tangible safeguard amid the collapse of centralised monetary authority and rampant inflation. These examples highlight that holding metals is often a practical expression of ethical self-determination.

The moral appeal of metals also resonates with contemporary concerns about transparency and sustainability. Financial scandals—from corporate fraud to market manipulation—have eroded public confidence in conventional assets and institutions. Meanwhile, issues surrounding the provenance of metals—such as conflict minerals and environmentally destructive mining practices—raise important ethical questions. Responsible investing in precious metals today requires attention to sourcing, certification, and environmental impact, prompting investors to engage not only with financial value but with the ethical context of their holdings. This dimension enriches the notion of metals as "clean" value, suggesting that ethical investment demands both tangible assets and conscientious stewardship.

Furthermore, investing in gold and silver encourages a longer-term perspective often absent from fast-paced financial markets. The *philosophy of patience* inherent in precious metals ownership contrasts sharply with the short-termism and speculative frenzy common in equities or cryptocurrencies. This patience reflects an understanding of wealth as *capacity*—a reserve of value to be preserved across time, generations, and crises. It is an investment in *optionality*, the freedom to act without compulsion imposed by volatile markets or unstable institutions. This perspective embodies a moral clarity about the purpose of wealth: not merely consumption or status, but security, independence, and legacy.

Critics may argue that the absence of yield or dividends in metals challenges their viability as investments in a growth-oriented financial system. While this critique holds under conventional models prioritising income generation, it misses the broader ethical and strategic functions metals serve. They are not substitutes for growth assets but foundational components of resilient portfolios that balance ambition with prudence. Their value lies in preservation, trust, and *real* purchasing power rather than speculative gain. This distinction matters profoundly for investors attuned to the ethical implications of their choices.

The act of investing in precious metals thus becomes a statement about one's relationship with money and society. It acknowledges the limits of trust in financial intermediaries and recognises the fragility of modern monetary constructs. It affirms a commitment to tangible reality in an increasingly virtual economy. By choosing metals, investors align themselves with a tradition that prizes substance over shadow, permanence over pretense. This alignment is not merely financial but existential—a conscious affirmation of values amid uncertainty.

Understanding metals as moral assets reframes their role within broader economic and social frameworks. It challenges investors and policymakers alike to consider the ethical dimensions of wealth creation and preservation. This perspective invites a richer dialogue about what constitutes *legitimate* value and how financial systems can serve not only growth but justice, transparency, and sustainability.

Engaging with the moral metal invites readers to see precious metals as more than inert commodities or speculative tools. It calls for a reflective approach that honours their unique capacity to embody *clean value*—a rare commodity in contemporary finance. This insight deepens the discourse on investing, blending financial acumen with ethical clarity and philosophical depth.

Owning the Indestructible

In a financial world increasingly defined by volatility, abstraction, and impermanence, the appeal of gold and silver lies fundamentally in their *physical permanence*—a quality that distinguishes them sharply from most modern assets. While stocks fluctuate with market sentiment, bonds are subject to interest rate risk, and digital currencies exist solely as ephemeral entries on servers, precious metals remain tangible and enduring. This contrast is not merely technical; it carries profound emotional and strategic implications for those seeking long-term security. Owning gold and silver is, at its core, an act of acquiring something indestructible—wealth in a form that can withstand time, crisis, and uncertainty where other assets may fail.

The physicality of metals is central to their resilience. Gold and silver are elements that resist corrosion, decay, and degradation. Unlike paper money, which can be printed into oblivion, or digital assets vulnerable to hacking and technological obsolescence, metals exist independently of systems and infrastructures. They do not depend on the solvency of institutions, the reliability of networks, or the stability of governments. This *independence from context* endows metals with a unique durability. Historical artefacts composed of gold have survived thousands of years, maintaining their lustre and form through upheavals that erased entire empires and currencies. Such longevity offers not only a store of economic value but a *psychological anchor* amid the transient nature of contemporary finance.

Modern investors face an array of ephemeral assets—derivatives, cryptocurrencies, and paper instruments—that promise returns yet carry complex layers of risk, counterparty dependencies, and regulatory uncertainty. These innovations undoubtedly have their place in diversified portfolios, yet their fragility becomes apparent during times of systemic stress. The collapse of Lehman Brothers in 2008, flash crashes in electronic markets, and high-profile cryptocurrency exchange failures reveal vulnerabilities intrinsic to these intangible forms of wealth. By contrast, gold and silver do not rely on trust in digital platforms or corporate balance sheets; their value is rooted in *matter itself*. Owning a physical ounce of metal means possessing wealth that cannot be deleted, frozen, or diluted by policy.

This permanence also fosters a distinctive emotional security. The act of physically holding gold or silver appeals to primal instincts for safety and control. Studies in behavioural economics and psychology highlight how tangible assets can reduce anxiety and promote a sense of mastery over financial fate. The knowledge that one's wealth exists in a palpable, indestructible form resonates deeply, especially during periods of uncertainty—be it economic crises, geopolitical conflict, or technological disruption. This emotional dimension complements the strategic rationale for metals ownership, creating a holistic form of security that encompasses both mind and material.

Strategically, the indestructibility of metals aligns with the principle of *wealth preservation*. While other assets may offer income or growth potential, precious metals primarily serve as a bulwark against erosion—be it through inflation, currency devaluation, or institutional failure. Their enduring physical nature ensures that value is not subject to the whims of fiscal policy or market speculation. For investors concerned with legacy and intergenerational wealth transfer, metals offer a tangible means of passing down real purchasing power across centuries. This capacity to endure the passage of time elevates metals from mere commodities to foundational assets within a prudent financial plan.

Real-world applications reinforce this strategic value. During the hyperinflation of the 1920s Weimar Republic, paper marks became worthless, yet gold and silver retained their value. In the financial turmoil of the 2008 crisis, gold prices surged as investors sought refuge from collapsing credit markets. More recently, amid growing concerns over currency debasement and systemic risk, central banks worldwide have increased gold reserves, reaffirming metals as pillars of financial stability. These examples illustrate that owning the indestructible is not theoretical but a tested response to economic volatility and uncertainty.

However, the permanence of gold and silver also invites reflection on the nature of value itself. In a digital age where money often exists as fleeting bits and bytes, metals anchor wealth in a material reality that transcends virtual constructs. This tangibility challenges assumptions that value must be fast, liquid, and electronically mediated. Instead, it posits that *true security* may reside in slower, more deliberate forms of wealth—assets that are resilient precisely because they are resistant to technological and systemic fragility.

Critics may point to the lack of yield or the costs associated with storage and security as drawbacks of owning physical metals. While these considerations are valid, they must be weighed against the unparalleled security that permanence provides. Ownership of gold and silver is less about short-term gains and more about *strategic durability*. The emotional and financial insurance offered by indestructible assets justifies the investment in safeguarding them. Moreover, advancements in secure storage, insurance, and transport have mitigated many logistical challenges, making physical ownership increasingly practical for a range of investors.

The indestructible nature of metals also invites a broader philosophical stance on wealth. It encourages investors to think beyond transient market cycles and short-lived financial products, fostering a mindset oriented toward *sustainability, legacy, and resilience.* This long-term perspective aligns with fundamental human concerns: preserving resources for future generations, maintaining autonomy in uncertain times, and valuing substance over form. By embracing metals as indestructible wealth, investors engage not only with markets but with enduring principles of security and stewardship.

In synthesising these insights, it becomes clear that owning gold and silver is far more than a financial decision; it is an affirmation of permanence amid impermanence, a tangible commitment to preserving value that transcends time and turmoil. Their physical permanence contrasts starkly with the ephemeral nature of most contemporary assets, offering both emotional reassurance and strategic advantage. This dual function positions precious metals as indispensable components of a resilient portfolio—anchors in an ever-shifting economic sea, embodiments of wealth that can withstand not only market volatility but the ravages of history itself.

Owning the indestructible, then, is an act that blends the rational with the existential. It acknowledges the realities of modern finance while affirming a deeper human desire: to secure something lasting, reliable, and real. For those seeking clarity, confidence, and true long-term security, gold and silver stand unmatched—not just as metals, but as *monuments to permanence* in a fleeting world.

Chapter 3
When to Choose Metals Over Markets

In the sprawling, often unpredictable realm of modern finance, the question of when to favour precious metals over conventional markets is far from straightforward. Financial landscapes pulse with a torrent of signals—macroeconomic fluctuations, geopolitical tremors, inflationary currents—that can unsettle even the most experienced investor. Yet amid this apparent chaos lies a discernible rhythm, a subtle cadence of economic shifts and human behaviour that, if carefully observed, can indicate the moments when gold and silver serve not merely as assets, but as refuge. This chapter explores the art and science of interpreting these cues, providing readers with a framework to navigate uncertainty with both clarity and conviction.

One guiding principle here is the notion of reading the economic climate. Much like seasoned sailors who interpret skies, tides, and winds to chart safe passage, investors can learn to decode the indicators that presage market turbulence. Moves in monetary policy—sharp interest rate hikes or unconventional easing measures—often signal underlying fragility. Geopolitical tensions, from trade skirmishes to armed conflict, introduce volatility that frequently pushes metals into bullish territory. Likewise, sudden inflationary pressures, which erode purchasing power and unsettle confidence in currency, typically spur demand for tangible assets. By attuning to these markers, investors can anticipate turning points rather than respond belatedly.

Yet market dynamics are rarely dictated by economic logic alone. The emotional undercurrents—the so-called fear index—play an equally vital role. Anxiety over systemic collapse, geopolitical crises, or runaway inflation can rapidly propel metals from steady stores of value into vehicles of speculative intensity. Recognising when fear dominates market sentiment transforms panic-induced surges into potential opportunities, allowing judicious entry at moments of heightened anxiety rather than succumbing to herd impulses. Timing, in this context, demands psychological acuity as much as economic insight.

Adding further complexity is the recognition that precious metals move in discernible cycles and seasons, patterns shaped by long-term historical rhythms rather than day-to-day headlines. Gold and silver exhibit recurring performance trends relative to equities, bonds, and currencies—patterns that stretch across decades, even centuries. These cycles do not guarantee perfect timing, for such certainty remains elusive, but they provide a framework for strategic positioning. Understanding these rhythms encourages a measured approach, discouraging frantic attempts at precision while fostering alignment with broader market phases.

Underlying this analysis is a crucial question of intent: are metals being sought as a hedge against short-term volatility, or as a haven in anticipation of profound systemic disruption? Hedging mitigates immediate fluctuations, cushioning portfolios through episodic shocks. Investing for haven status, by contrast, positions metals as anchors against structural shifts that could redefine financial norms. Clarifying this purpose avoids reactionary hoarding born of fear, instead promoting strategies aligned with one's risk appetite, temporal horizon, and philosophical outlook.

Throughout this chapter, readers encounter more than technical instruction; they engage with the intertwined realities of precious metals investing, where economics, psychology, history, and strategy converge. By integrating rigorous analysis with an appreciation of human behaviour and historical precedent, the chapter equips investors to discern when metals are the prudent choice over conventional markets. In an era where economic stability is increasingly fragile and traditional instruments face unprecedented pressures, this knowledge proves indispensable.

Ultimately, investing in metals is less about reactive shelter and more about deliberate, informed discernment—understanding systemic signals, recognising emotional dynamics, and interpreting cyclical patterns. Mastery lies not in chasing momentary gains, but in perceiving the deeper currents beneath surface volatility, balancing rational analysis with human insight, and aligning action with intent. This chapter provides the tools for such mastery, offering depth, clarity, and actionable wisdom for those prepared to navigate uncertainty with purpose and strategic foresight.

Reading the Economic Weather: Signals of Systemic Risk

The ability to anticipate shifts in the financial landscape is a skill of immense value, especially when it comes to recognising the early signs that often precede bull runs in precious metals. Unlike speculative trends driven purely by momentum, metals' price movements frequently respond to *systemic risk*—the latent stresses accumulating beneath the surface of economies and markets. Reading these signals effectively requires a nuanced understanding of macroeconomic indicators, geopolitical dynamics, and inflationary pressures that collectively form the economic weather. This article equips readers with a framework for discerning these signals, empowering them to position gold and silver strategically before widespread recognition triggers market rallies.

Monetary policy stands at the forefront of these macro indicators. Central banks wield profound influence over economies through interest rates, quantitative easing, and balance sheet management. When policymakers lower interest rates aggressively or embark on expansive asset purchase programmes, they inject liquidity into markets, often to counteract economic slowdowns or crises. While these actions can stabilise short-term conditions, they also sow the seeds of longer-term risks—excessive credit growth, asset bubbles, and currency debasement. History shows that such expansive monetary policies often coincide with rising metals prices. For example, the Federal Reserve's response to the 2008 financial crisis involved unprecedented quantitative easing that eventually propelled gold to new highs. Understanding the subtle shifts in central bank rhetoric, policy decisions, and inflation targeting frameworks can provide early clues about the trajectory of metals markets.

Equally important is the assessment of geopolitical unrest, which acts as a catalyst amplifying systemic vulnerabilities. Conflicts, trade wars, sanctions, and diplomatic tensions introduce uncertainty and risk that undermine confidence in conventional assets and currencies. The metals market, by contrast, often benefits from such instability as investors seek *safe havens* immune to political disruption. The invasion of Crimea in 2014, escalating US-China trade tensions in 2018, and Middle Eastern conflicts have all contributed to spikes in gold and silver demand. Geopolitical risk is multifaceted and can manifest in sudden crises or prolonged instability, requiring investors to maintain vigilance and contextual awareness. Interpreting these events within broader economic trends distinguishes momentary noise from genuine systemic alarms.

Inflationary pressures present another critical signal of systemic risk with direct implications for metals. Inflation erodes purchasing power and shakes confidence in fiat currencies, prompting investors to seek assets that preserve value. Yet not all inflation is equal; understanding the drivers—be they supply chain disruptions, commodity price shocks, or expansive fiscal policies—is essential. The inflation surge experienced globally post-2020, driven by pandemic-related disruptions and stimulus spending, triggered renewed interest in gold and silver. Crucially, markets often price in inflation expectations before headline figures confirm rising prices, making indicators like breakeven inflation rates, commodity futures, and wage trends vital tools. Investors who interpret these nuances can anticipate metals' responses with greater precision.

Beyond individual indicators, systemic risk emerges from the *interaction* of these forces. For instance, accommodative monetary policy combined with geopolitical tensions and rising inflation creates a perfect storm for metals bull markets. The 1970s stagflation era exemplifies how intertwined economic stagnation, inflation, and political crises propelled gold prices dramatically. Contemporary parallels, including debt saturation, trade disputes, and inflationary fears, suggest that systemic vulnerabilities often cluster, intensifying their impact. Recognising such convergence is pivotal for discerning when metals move from safe harbour to strategic asset.

The complexity of systemic risk also demands a critical perspective on consensus narratives. Markets and policymakers may downplay risks to maintain stability or avoid panic, masking true vulnerabilities until they surface abruptly. The 2008 crisis illustrated how hidden leverage and interdependencies can catch even experienced observers unprepared. Metals' traditional role as an early warning indicator—often rising in price before crises become apparent—positions them uniquely as barometers of economic health. Investors attentive to anomalies in credit spreads, currency behaviours, or unconventional monetary measures gain an informational edge, positioning metals before widespread recognition fuels price surges.

Practical application of this knowledge requires synthesising diverse data points into coherent signals without succumbing to paralysis by analysis. Developing an intuitive grasp of economic weather patterns emerges from continuous observation and contextualisation. Monitoring central bank meetings, geopolitical developments, inflation reports, and financial market indicators collectively sharpens insight. For example, a sudden pivot in Federal Reserve communication combined with escalating geopolitical tensions and inflation exceeding forecasts would strongly suggest growing systemic risk—prompting a reassessment of metals' role in one's portfolio.

Moreover, recognising *timing* nuances is crucial. Metals often begin to appreciate well before crises peak, rewarding proactive positioning. Yet premature or excessive exposure can lead to opportunity costs. Thus, understanding the economic weather entails balancing vigilance with patience—knowing when to increase metals' weight strategically and when to maintain or reduce exposure based on evolving signals.

Reading systemic risk also intersects with understanding human psychology and market dynamics. Fear and uncertainty drive flight to safety, yet markets can overshoot or react prematurely. Metals markets are influenced not only by fundamental signals but also by sentiment and speculation. Integrating quantitative indicators with qualitative assessments of market mood, media narratives, and investor behaviour enhances decision-making depth.

Finally, this approach aligns with broader themes of intentional investing emphasised throughout this book. It shifts metals investment from reactive to strategic—grounded in an informed reading of macro conditions rather than impulsive responses. It respects the complexity of global systems and the unpredictability of crises, advocating a disciplined, evidence-based engagement with precious metals as part of a comprehensive risk management framework.

In mastering the art of reading economic weather, investors gain more than technical skill; they cultivate *foresight*, a quality essential for navigating the uncertainties of contemporary finance. This foresight empowers prudent allocation to precious metals, enhancing resilience and positioning for opportunity in the face of systemic upheaval. The insights offered here represent a cornerstone of sophisticated metals investing—a guide to interpreting the subtle signals that precede market transformation and to harnessing metals' enduring role as guardians of value.

The Fear Index: When Emotion Drives Price

The markets are often portrayed as arenas of rational calculation, where price reflects the collective wisdom of countless informed participants weighing risk and reward. Yet beneath this veneer of logic lies a powerful and enduring force that frequently eclipses reason: *fear*. In the metals market, fear—whether of economic collapse, geopolitical conflict, or runaway inflation—has repeatedly dictated price movements with a force and immediacy that defies purely analytical explanation. Understanding how fear shapes the valuation of gold and silver is essential for discerning investors who wish to navigate the metals markets with both clarity and strategic acumen. Recognising when fear drives prices is not merely academic; it offers the opportunity to *transform panic into advantage*.

The emotional dynamics underpinning metals markets are rooted in the nature of gold and silver themselves. These metals have historically been viewed as *safe havens*, assets that retain value when conventional investments falter. This reputation elevates them beyond mere commodities to psychological anchors during periods of uncertainty. When fears mount—whether triggered by financial crises, wars, or inflationary spirals—investors flock to metals as refuges. The resulting surge in demand often outpaces fundamental economic shifts, leading to price spikes that reflect collective anxiety as much as tangible value. This phenomenon underscores a key insight: metals prices do not merely respond to logical calculations but are deeply intertwined with the *sentiment and psychology* of market participants.

Fear's influence on metal prices is vividly illustrated during episodes of acute crisis. The 2008 global financial meltdown offers a paradigmatic example. As confidence in banks and credit markets eroded, gold prices soared, driven largely by panic-induced buying. Investors sought to preserve wealth amid collapsing asset classes, pushing gold from around $800 an ounce in 2007 to over $1,900 by 2011. This dramatic rise outstripped traditional valuation models, reflecting the emotional contagion spreading through markets. Similar patterns emerged during the COVID-19 pandemic, when uncertainty about economic stability and monetary policy prompted another surge in gold and silver prices. These episodes reveal that metals markets are *emotional barometers*, sensitive to fear's ebb and flow.

Yet, fear-driven markets are not unidimensional. They encapsulate a complex interplay of rational and irrational factors. While fear can trigger *legitimate flight to safety* in response to real risks, it can also provoke *overreactions* and speculative bubbles. Prices may rise beyond levels justified by fundamentals, creating volatility that challenges even seasoned investors. Recognising this duality is crucial. Effective engagement with the fear index demands an ability to distinguish between justified caution and emotional excess—a skill that requires both analytical rigor and psychological insight.

Understanding the mechanisms by which fear propagates in markets illuminates how panic can become opportunity. Fear often manifests through behavioural biases: herd mentality, loss aversion, and overestimation of rare but catastrophic events. These biases drive rapid shifts in buying and selling behaviour, magnifying price movements. For instance, during geopolitical crises such as the Gulf War or the annexation of Crimea, gold prices experienced swift rallies fueled by uncertainty and risk aversion rather than immediate economic disruption. Investors who recognise these signals early can position themselves advantageously, entering markets when prices reflect fear's peak rather than its onset or resolution.

Contrasting perspectives enrich this analysis. Some argue that fear-driven price spikes undermine metals' role as stable stores of value, introducing unnecessary volatility and speculative risk. Others contend that such price action is integral to metals' function as hedges, reflecting the realignment of risk preferences in turbulent times. This tension highlights the need for a nuanced understanding that neither dismisses nor romanticises fear's role but situates it within a broader framework of market dynamics and investor psychology.

Practical application of this understanding involves monitoring *leading indicators* of fear and market sentiment. Volatility indices, credit spreads, political developments, and inflation expectations serve as early warning signals. Media narratives and social sentiment analyses further reveal shifts in collective mood that precede metals market reactions. For example, spikes in the VIX (volatility index) have historically correlated with rising gold demand, while widening credit spreads signal growing economic stress that often benefits metals. Incorporating these tools enhances the investor's ability to anticipate fear-driven price movements and act with informed timing.

Moreover, recognising the emotional drivers behind metals markets invites reflection on the investor's own psychology. Fear can lead to reactive, impulsive decisions—buying at peaks or selling in despair—that undermine long-term outcomes. Cultivating emotional discipline and a strategic mindset transforms fear from a source of disruption into a lens for opportunity. Investors who master this balance avoid the pitfalls of panic while harnessing metals' protective qualities.

Beyond individual markets, the fear index phenomenon intersects with broader societal and ethical considerations. In times of widespread uncertainty, the collective turn to metals reflects deeper anxieties about trust in institutions, currencies, and global stability. This dynamic underscores the sociopolitical significance of metals as *symbols of security*—their rising prices communicating shared concerns and priorities. Recognising this social dimension adds layers of insight to the investor's understanding, situating metals within the currents of history and human behaviour.

Engaging with the fear index thus equips investors not only with market knowledge but with a richer appreciation of the psychological and social forces shaping value. It reveals metals markets as complex arenas where logic and emotion intertwine, where panic may obscure but also create opportunity. This awareness fosters a more sophisticated, resilient approach to metals investing—one that respects fear's power while transcending its distortions.

In mastering when and how fear moves metals, investors gain a vital tool for navigating uncertainty. They learn to read the subtle signals of panic, to differentiate transient spikes from sustained trends, and to position wealth with both prudence and confidence. This skill transforms metals investing from reactive to anticipatory, from vulnerable to empowered. Understanding the fear index is, therefore, not merely an academic exercise but a practical imperative for those seeking to secure value amid the unpredictable tides of global finance.

Cycles and Seasons: Gold's Rhythms Across Time

In the realm of investing, few assets display the rhythmic cadence of gold and silver. Unlike stocks or bonds, whose values often rise or fall in response to company earnings, interest rates, or fiscal policies, precious metals move according to broader economic and psychological cycles that have persisted for centuries. Recognising these *cycles and seasons* is not about precise market timing—a notoriously elusive goal—but about understanding the underlying rhythms that govern metals' relative performance. This awareness enables investors to position themselves with greater confidence and strategic foresight, embracing gold and silver as components of a long-term portfolio that navigates markets not through guesswork, but through informed rhythm.

Historical data demonstrates that gold and silver have exhibited cyclical behaviour tightly intertwined with macroeconomic conditions, geopolitical developments, and shifts in monetary regimes. For example, the post-World War II period saw metals subdued under the Bretton Woods system, which fixed currencies to the dollar and the dollar to gold. Only after the system's collapse in 1971 did gold embark on a prolonged bull run that lasted through much of the 1970s, a decade marked by inflation, oil shocks, and geopolitical upheaval. Silver, often more volatile, mirrored these movements, amplifying metals' role as hedges against monetary instability and economic uncertainty. Understanding these historical arcs reveals that metals' cycles often reflect the broader *economic seasons*—periods of stability, inflation, crisis, and recalibration—that define financial history.

Comparing metals' performance to traditional assets like stocks and bonds further illuminates their cyclical nature. Equities tend to thrive during growth and recovery phases, benefiting from expanding corporate profits and consumer confidence. Bonds, depending on interest rate trends, can offer stability but are vulnerable to inflationary pressures. Metals, conversely, frequently excel during *risk-off* periods—when markets grapple with inflation, geopolitical risks, or currency devaluation. This inverse relationship underscores metals' function as portfolio stabilisers. For example, during the dot-com bubble burst and the 2008 financial crisis, gold's value increased even as equities tumbled, demonstrating its countercyclical strength. Recognising these patterns allows investors to anticipate when metals might outperform relative to other asset classes without relying on exact timing.

Cycles in precious metals also intersect with monetary policy trends and inflation expectations. Historically, periods of expansive monetary policy and rising inflation coincide with metals' upward phases. The 1970s inflation surge, the early 2000s commodity boom, and post-2008 quantitative easing cycles exemplify this relationship. However, metals are not immune to secular shifts. Extended periods of disinflation or monetary tightening can temper metals' performance, as seen in the 1980s and 1990s. Thus, appreciating the *seasonal* aspect of metals involves tracking monetary cycles and inflation dynamics over multiple years rather than reacting to short-term fluctuations.

Silver's cycles often exhibit greater volatility and magnified moves relative to gold, reflecting its dual role as a precious metal and an industrial commodity. During commodity booms, silver prices can soar beyond typical precious metals trends, while industrial downturns may depress its value disproportionately. This duality adds nuance to silver's seasonal patterns, requiring investors to consider both monetary and industrial demand drivers in their timing assessments.

A critical insight from metals' cyclical nature is the futility of attempting to *time the market* precisely. Instead, a more effective approach is to understand the broad contours of metals' cycles and to make strategic, phased entries aligned with macroeconomic and market signals. This method reduces emotional decision-making and helps avoid costly errors born of impatience or speculation. Long-term investors benefit from recognising metals' seasons as part of a diversified strategy that balances growth assets with stable stores of value.

Beyond economics, metals' cycles resonate with human psychology and behaviour. Periods of fear and uncertainty tend to amplify demand for gold and silver, while complacency and confidence can suppress it. These collective sentiments often unfold in waves, reflecting broader social moods and risk appetites. Investing with awareness of these emotional cycles adds depth to technical and fundamental analysis, integrating the human element that drives market rhythms.

Case studies illustrate how cyclical understanding has practical applications. The gold price surge following the 2008 crisis was not a sudden anomaly but the culmination of deteriorating monetary conditions and rising risk aversion over several years. Investors who recognised early signs—such as expanding central bank balance sheets, credit market stresses, and geopolitical tensions—were better positioned to capitalise on metals' rally. Similarly, the prolonged metals downturn from 2011 to 2015 coincided with stabilising inflation and tightening monetary policy, marking a seasonal trough. These examples underscore the value of cyclical literacy in metals investing.

Integrating metals' cycles with broader portfolio construction enhances risk management and return potential. By adjusting metals' allocation according to anticipated economic seasons—ramping up exposure during inflationary or crisis phases and moderating it during stable growth—investors harness metals' defensive attributes without sacrificing participation in growth markets. This dynamic approach acknowledges the rhythms of global finance rather than fighting them.

The concept of cycles and seasons also invites philosophical reflection on time and value. Precious metals, with their longevity and historical continuity, embody a rhythm of *endurance* that contrasts with the rapid churn of modern financial markets. Embracing their cycles is an act of aligning investment strategy with enduring economic realities and human behavioural patterns, fostering patience and perspective in an often frenetic investment environment.

Ultimately, understanding gold and silver's rhythms across time equips investors with a powerful framework to engage metals markets thoughtfully and effectively. It transcends the illusion of perfect timing, offering instead a disciplined, informed path that respects the complex interplay of economic forces and human psychology. This insight transforms metals investing from guesswork into a deliberate practice grounded in history, analysis, and wisdom—essential qualities for securing and growing wealth in a world defined by uncertainty and change.

Hedge or Haven? Clarifying Your Intent

In the complex landscape of investing in precious metals, one of the most crucial distinctions an investor must make is between using gold and silver as a *hedge* against short-term volatility and as a *haven* in preparation for long-term systemic disruption. This distinction is not merely semantic; it fundamentally shapes strategy, risk management, and ultimately, the value derived from metals ownership. Too often, investors conflate these purposes, reacting impulsively to market turbulence with uncalculated hoarding rather than deliberate, purpose-driven allocation. Clarifying one's intent transforms metals investing from a reflexive act into a coherent, resilient financial strategy.

A *hedge* functions as a protective mechanism against foreseeable, temporary market fluctuations. Investors employ metals as hedges to cushion portfolios from inflation spikes, currency weakness, or short-lived geopolitical shocks. This use is tactical and typically involves modest allocations designed to offset specific risks within a diversified portfolio. For instance, an investor concerned about rising inflation over the coming months may increase exposure to gold or silver to preserve purchasing power during that window. This form of hedging recognises metals as *instruments of risk management*, responsive to economic indicators and market cycles, but not necessarily as a permanent core holding.

Conversely, a *haven* implies a more profound role—metals held as anchors amid anticipated structural changes or crises that could upend conventional financial systems. This approach is strategic and philosophical, reflecting an understanding that fiat currencies and traditional markets can fail, erode, or collapse over time. Investors who view metals as havens allocate with a long horizon, often accepting volatility and illiquidity in exchange for the enduring security metals confer. Historical examples reinforce this stance: during hyperinflations, regime changes, or systemic banking failures, gold and silver have preserved wealth when other assets became worthless. Thus, owning metals as havens aligns with an existential imperative to safeguard *real, tangible value* beyond transient market conditions.

The tension between these two approaches—hedging versus havening—reveals essential questions about risk perception and investment objectives. Hedge-driven investing tends to be reactive, tied to observable threats and market noise. It can lead to cyclical buying and selling, often mistimed due to emotional responses. Haven-oriented investing demands patience, conviction, and a holistic view that anticipates deep uncertainties rather than short-term disruptions. It involves resisting the temptation to overreact to headline volatility and instead maintaining metals as foundational wealth components designed to withstand profound upheavals.

Clarifying intent also influences practical considerations such as allocation size, asset form, and storage strategy. Hedging might warrant smaller allocations through liquid instruments like ETFs or allocated bullion, enabling rapid adjustment. Haven investing often requires larger holdings of physical metals, securely stored and diversified geographically, to ensure control and accessibility under crisis conditions. Recognising these distinctions prevents the common pitfall of accumulating metals impulsively in response to fear, which can result in overexposure, liquidity constraints, and missed opportunities in other asset classes.

This differentiation is not merely academic but deeply practical. The 2008 financial crisis and the COVID-19 pandemic highlight how metals functioned both as tactical hedges—rising amid immediate turmoil—and as havens, underpinning wealth preservation beyond the initial shocks. Investors who treated metals purely as hedges often struggled with timing exits and re-entries, while those embracing metals as havens maintained stability and confidence throughout prolonged uncertainty. This historical perspective underscores the strategic advantage of purpose-driven investing.

Ethical and philosophical reflections further enrich this discourse. Investing with clear intent in metals acknowledges the limitations of conventional financial systems and the moral imperative to preserve *clean, enduring value.* It rejects the reactive accumulation driven by panic or herd behaviour, promoting instead a disciplined, thoughtful engagement with metals as a form of financial sovereignty. This mindset fosters resilience not only in portfolios but in the investor's relationship with risk, uncertainty, and time.

The distinction between hedge and haven also aligns with broader portfolio construction principles. Metals as hedges complement growth assets by smoothing volatility and providing insurance against inflationary surprises. As havens, metals form the backbone of a portfolio's defensive core, offering protection when systemic shocks render other assets illiquid or devalued. Balancing these roles requires continuous reassessment of macroeconomic trends, geopolitical risks, and personal circumstances, reinforcing metals' dynamic function rather than static categorisation.

Ultimately, clarifying one's intent when investing in precious metals transforms the process from reaction to strategy. It fosters a purpose-driven approach that integrates metals coherently within financial plans, aligning risk management with philosophical clarity. This clarity enables investors to harness metals' unique strengths—whether as timely hedges against market gyrations or as steadfast havens guarding wealth through deep uncertainty—maximising their enduring value amid the complexities of modern finance.

Chapter 4
The Physical Truth—Holding Gold in Your Hands

There is a distinctive gravity in the act of holding gold—its weight in the hand, the glint of metal catching the light—an immediacy of value that no ledger entry or digital token can replicate. As modern finance drifts ever further into the intangible, the physical presence of precious metals asserts a clarity and certainty increasingly rare. This chapter undertakes a detailed exploration of what it genuinely means to own gold and silver, cutting through the mystique of bullion, bars, and coins to reveal the practical, strategic, and philosophical truths of possession. For investors intent on anchoring wealth in something real, mastering the material aspects of metals is indispensable.

The journey begins with a careful survey of the forms in which precious metals are bought and held. Gold and silver present themselves as sovereign coins, minted bars of varying weights, and investment-grade rounds—each designed to suit distinct purposes. Sovereign coins, such as the American Gold Eagle, Canadian Maple Leaf, or British Britannia, carry legal tender status, widespread recognition, and high liquidity, making them favoured by those seeking trusted authenticity and ease of trade. By contrast, kilo bars or larger ingots tend to attract institutional buyers or those prioritising cost efficiency, as bulk purchases usually carry lower premiums above spot prices. This chapter unpacks these options with clarity, guiding readers to match format with objective—whether that be long-term storage, ready liquidation, or even gifting.

Ownership, however, extends beyond selection. It demands acute attention to purity, premiums, and hidden pitfalls that influence real value. Purity, expressed in fineness such as .9999 for gold, determines intrinsic metal content; premiums above spot price reflect minting, distribution, and dealer markups. Navigating this terrain requires vigilance: overpaying for speculative collectibles, falling prey to unscrupulous sellers, or acquiring counterfeit products are persistent risks. Evaluating premiums with informed judgment protects returns, yet occasionally higher premiums are justified by provenance, liquidity, or storage convenience. This chapter equips readers with the tools to critically assess offers, understanding how subtle variations in purity and cost translate into real economic value.

Equally crucial is knowing how to acquire metals safely. The proliferation of online marketplaces, private dealers, auctions, and peer-to-peer sales presents unprecedented access—but also magnifies risk. Trustworthiness and transparency are non-negotiable. Reputable dealers offer certification, secure logistics, and clear return policies; the lure of low prices on unfamiliar platforms can swiftly prove costly. The chapter outlines best practices for due diligence: verifying credentials, understanding grading systems, leveraging industry associations, and recognising the importance of physical inspection and provenance documentation. These measures ensure that acquisition strengthens, rather than undermines, the security of ownership.

Bringing theory to life, the chapter intersperses anecdotal narratives from seasoned investors. These stories illuminate the challenges and lessons of physical metals ownership: misjudged storage risks, timing decisions amid market swings, and the emotional heft of safeguarding assets during crises. One investor recounts narrowly avoiding a counterfeit purchase through meticulous authentication; another describes the tranquillity derived from offshore vault storage during political uncertainty. Such vignettes underscore that owning gold and silver is not a mere transaction—it is an active relationship requiring trust, vigilance, and intention.

Underlying these practicalities is a profound philosophical resonance. Holding gold and silver connects one to a lineage of tangible wealth spanning generations and continents. The physicality of metal anchors abstract financial concepts in reality, offering a bulwark against digital fragility and institutional failure. This material permanence conveys confidence, dignity, and sovereignty, affirming the owner's control over an indestructible asset. For many, this connection surpasses numeric calculations, addressing deeper human desires for stability, authenticity, and resilience.

In essence, this chapter delivers a comprehensive guide to the tangible realities of precious metals ownership. Balancing technical exactitude with strategic insight and human perspective, it empowers readers to approach metals with competence and confidence. By examining forms, costs, acquisition methods, and lived experiences, it transforms ownership from abstract notion to practical engagement—laying the foundation for a secure, intentional, and enduring relationship with these elemental repositories of value.

Bullion, Bars, and Coins: What to Actually Buy

In the world of precious metals investing, the seemingly simple question of *what to buy* quickly unfolds into a complex landscape of options, each with unique characteristics, advantages, and challenges. The physical forms of gold and silver—ranging from sovereign coins to kilo bars—are not interchangeable commodities but carefully crafted instruments tailored to different investor goals, risk appetites, and logistical considerations. Understanding these distinctions is essential for making informed choices that align with one's financial objectives and practical realities. This article navigates the nuances of bullion, bars, and coins, demystifying their roles and guiding investors toward selections that best serve their purposes.

Bullion represents the foundational category of precious metals investment: refined metal cast into standardized shapes and weights, valued primarily for its metal content rather than collectible or artistic merit. Bullion's appeal lies in its purity, liquidity, and relative cost-efficiency. It is commonly produced in forms such as bars, rounds, and coins, with purity typically at or above 99.5% for silver and 99.99% for gold. This purity standard ensures that bullion maintains intrinsic value, independent of fluctuating market fashions or numismatic trends. For investors focused on long-term wealth preservation and straightforward value storage, bullion offers a reliable, transparent medium.

Bars, often synonymous with bullion but distinguished by their shape and scale, come in a variety of sizes—from small one-gram increments to large kilo bars and beyond. Smaller bars offer flexibility, allowing investors to build positions incrementally or liquidate portions without disrupting their entire holding. Larger bars, while generally commanding lower premiums per ounce due to economies of scale, require considerations around storage, security, and liquidity. For example, kilo bars are popular among institutional investors or serious private holders who prioritise cost efficiency and long-term storage. However, the trade-off often lies in reduced ease of sale, particularly in markets favouring smaller denominations. Understanding this balance between size, liquidity, and cost is critical in bar selection.

Coins introduce a distinct dimension to precious metals ownership. Unlike generic bars, coins are minted with official markings, legal tender status, and often feature intricate designs that carry cultural and historical significance. Sovereign coins such as the American Gold Eagle, Canadian Maple Leaf, or South African Krugerrand have established global reputations, facilitating ease of resale and acceptance across markets. Their recognisability enhances liquidity and investor confidence. Moreover, legal tender status can confer tax advantages in certain jurisdictions, further incentivising their use. Yet, coins typically command higher premiums due to minting costs and demand, a factor that must be weighed against their benefits. Collectors' coins or limited editions can carry substantial numismatic premiums but introduce complexity and risk unrelated to metal value, making them unsuitable for most investors seeking pure metal exposure.

Matching physical form to investment goal requires clarity of purpose. For those prioritising *cost efficiency* and bulk storage, generic bars provide an optimal solution. Conversely, investors seeking *ease of transaction*, portability, and widespread recognition often favour sovereign coins. Smaller investors or those beginning their metals journey may find fractional coins or smaller bars advantageous for flexibility. This alignment is not static; as portfolios grow or market conditions evolve, transitioning between forms may become prudent. For instance, an investor might accumulate small coins initially for liquidity and gradually consolidate into larger bars for cost savings.

Critical to navigating this landscape is an understanding of *premiums*—the additional costs above the spot price of metal that reflect manufacturing, distribution, and dealer margins. Premiums vary significantly between bars and coins, sizes, and market conditions. For example, a 1-ounce gold coin might carry a premium of 3-5%, whereas a kilo bar's premium might be less than 1%. Silver premiums tend to fluctuate more widely due to industrial demand and supply factors. Awareness of premium structures prevents overpaying and enhances return potential. Moreover, recognising that premiums can expand during market stress or supply constraints underscores the importance of timing and sourcing.

The issue of authenticity and provenance further differentiates physical forms. Officially minted coins carry government guarantees and often include anti-counterfeiting features such as micro-engraving or holograms. Bars from reputable refiners are stamped with assay marks certifying purity and weight, a crucial factor in resale and verification. Conversely, generic rounds or privately minted pieces require greater scrutiny and trusted intermediaries to avoid counterfeit risk. This dimension elevates the importance of buying from reputable dealers and institutions, particularly for novices. The trade-off between convenience, cost, and security is a recurring theme in form selection.

Storage considerations influence the choice of physical form as well. Smaller coins and bars offer portability and easier concealment, appealing to investors prioritising personal control and access. Larger bars necessitate secure vault storage, often incurring additional costs but offering enhanced security and insurance options. Some investors adopt a blended approach, holding a mix of sizes and forms to balance liquidity, security, and cost. This diversification within metals holdings complements broader portfolio strategies.

The practical realities of buying and selling also factor heavily into form choice. Sovereign coins enjoy broad acceptance among dealers and private buyers worldwide, facilitating smoother transactions. Bars, particularly those without widely recognised refinery marks, may encounter narrower markets and require verification at sale. This liquidity gradient informs exit planning, underscoring that form selection is not merely about acquisition but also about ease of future disposition.

Emerging market trends and innovations continue to shape metals ownership. Advances in digital certification, blockchain-based provenance tracking, and secure vaulting services enhance transparency and trust. These developments may reduce some traditional trade-offs between cost and security, broadening access and choice. Nonetheless, fundamental principles regarding form suitability remain relevant, demanding ongoing investor education and discernment.

Ultimately, the decision of what physical form of gold or silver to buy is a multidimensional one, reflecting individual objectives, risk tolerance, budget, and practical constraints. It resists simplistic answers or one-size-fits-all prescriptions. This complexity invites a measured, informed approach—one that respects the intrinsic qualities of bullion, bars, and coins while aligning them thoughtfully with the investor's unique context.

By demystifying the forms of precious metals and clarifying their respective roles, this chapter empowers readers to move beyond confusion and hesitation. It provides a foundation for confident, strategic choices that maximise metals' potential as vehicles of wealth preservation and financial sovereignty. Understanding what to actually buy transforms metals ownership from an abstract concept into a tangible, purposeful act—anchored in knowledge, foresight, and real-world practicality.

Purity, Premiums, and Pitfalls

Investing in physical gold and silver is often perceived as a straightforward endeavour: purchase a tangible asset and hold it as a store of value. Yet beneath this surface simplicity lies a landscape replete with complexities—where purity, premiums, and subtle pitfalls shape the *true cost* and ultimately the *value* of one's investment. To navigate this terrain effectively requires a keen understanding of the technical, economic, and practical factors that influence metals pricing and quality. This article unpacks these critical dimensions, equipping investors with the discernment needed to avoid common traps and make decisions rooted in clarity and confidence.

At the heart of physical metals valuation lies *purity*—the measure of metal content within an object, expressed as fineness or percentage. For gold, purity typically ranges from 91.7% (22 karat) to 99.99% (24 karat), with investment-grade bullion standardised at .9999 fine. Silver bullion generally maintains a purity of .999 or higher. Purity is not merely a technical specification; it directly determines the intrinsic value of the metal itself. Even fractional differences in fineness can translate into significant value disparities, especially at scale. Recognising purity's role is fundamental to assessing the authenticity and worth of any purchase.

However, purity alone does not dictate price. *Premiums*—the costs added above the spot price of the metal—play a decisive role in the actual expense incurred by buyers. Premiums encompass minting and manufacturing costs, distribution expenses, dealer margins, and market demand factors. These premiums vary widely based on form, size, brand recognition, and market conditions. For example, small gold coins often carry higher premiums per ounce than large bars due to increased manufacturing costs and greater liquidity. Conversely, kilo bars usually offer the lowest premiums, reflecting production efficiencies. Silver premiums tend to fluctuate more with market supply-demand imbalances and industrial demand, leading to sometimes volatile cost structures.

Understanding premiums requires scrutiny beyond headline prices. Dealers may quote spot-plus premiums that appear low, yet hidden fees—such as shipping, insurance, or storage charges—can elevate total costs. Seasonal demand spikes or geopolitical tensions often inflate premiums sharply, creating timing considerations for buyers. Notably, premiums can be significantly higher for numismatic or collectible coins, where rarity and historical value overshadow metal content. Investors prioritising pure metal exposure must differentiate between intrinsic and speculative value to avoid overpaying.

This intersection of purity and premiums exposes several *pitfalls* that ensnare even experienced investors. Counterfeits, misrepresented purity levels, and adulterated metals pose ongoing risks. Unscrupulous dealers may exploit buyers' inexperience by selling coins or bars with inflated premiums or dubious provenance. The secondary market's variability complicates valuation, particularly for less recognised products or non-sovereign items. Moreover, illiquid metals may be difficult to resell at expected prices, especially during market stress. These challenges highlight the necessity of comprehensive due diligence, including certification verification, reputable dealer selection, and understanding market liquidity.

The tension between cost-efficiency and security also surfaces in decisions about *form and brand.* Globally recognised refiners and mints—such as PAMP, Johnson Matthey, or governmental mints—offer products with established trust and recognisable marks, facilitating resale and reducing counterparty risk. While generic rounds and private mints may be cheaper upfront, they often lack this credibility, impacting liquidity and value stability. Investors must balance immediate cost savings against potential future hurdles, especially when metals are intended as long-term stores of value.

Evaluating the *true cost* of physical metals also involves considering storage and insurance. Holding metals privately entails safeguarding against theft, loss, or damage, which carries direct financial and emotional costs. Professional vault storage mitigates these risks but introduces recurring fees that reduce net returns. These expenses, while separate from purchase premiums, contribute to the comprehensive cost of ownership and must be incorporated into investment calculations.

Market dynamics further complicate the premium landscape. During periods of heightened uncertainty—financial crises, geopolitical upheavals, or supply chain disruptions—premiums can spike dramatically as demand outstrips supply. For example, during the 2020 pandemic onset, silver premiums surged as retail and industrial demand collided with constrained supply chains. Such episodes test investors' patience and timing, underscoring the importance of strategic accumulation rather than reactionary buying at peak premiums.

An essential yet often overlooked dimension is the *psychological impact* of premiums and perceived value. Investors may irrationally accept inflated premiums out of fear or urgency, inadvertently diminishing their returns. Conversely, fixation on obtaining the lowest premium can lead to excessive risk-taking or missed opportunities. Cultivating a balanced perspective—appreciating premiums as legitimate costs reflecting market realities rather than mere fees to be avoided—enhances decision-making quality.

Ethical considerations also arise in evaluating purity and sourcing. Concerns about "conflict metals," environmentally harmful mining practices, and labour standards prompt investors to seek certified, responsibly sourced bullion. Verification through recognised frameworks, such as the Responsible Jewellery Council or London Bullion Market Association accreditation, adds layers of assurance. This ethical dimension complements financial evaluation, aligning investment with broader values of sustainability and social responsibility.

The interaction of purity, premiums, and pitfalls converges in the critical practice of *due diligence.* This encompasses verifying assay certificates, consulting trusted price guides, understanding dealer reputations, and engaging with independent third-party experts where necessary. It requires ongoing education and vigilance, as market conditions, product offerings, and regulatory landscapes evolve. Investors who commit to rigorous due diligence position themselves to avoid costly mistakes and maximise the protective qualities of physical metals.

Case studies underscore these principles in action. One experienced investor recounts discovering counterfeit kilo bars purchased from an unreliable source, a costly lesson that prompted a thorough vetting process and exclusive reliance on accredited dealers. Another illustrates how ignorance of premiums led to overpayment on small silver rounds during a market spike, eroding expected gains. These narratives highlight that mastery of purity and premiums is not theoretical but central to preserving wealth and confidence.

In sum, evaluating the true cost and value of physical gold and silver demands more than cursory price comparisons or intuitive judgments. It calls for a disciplined, multifaceted approach that integrates technical knowledge of purity standards, keen awareness of premiums, cautious navigation of market pitfalls, and ethical considerations. This approach transforms metals investing from a gamble into a reasoned, strategic endeavour—one that honours the physical reality and enduring worth of precious metals while protecting investors from common hazards.

Armed with these insights, readers gain the clarity and confidence to approach physical metals purchases judiciously and intentionally. They learn to see beyond face value to the intricate cost structures that shape investment outcomes, to question assumptions, and to seek transparency and integrity in every transaction. This knowledge elevates metals ownership from mere possession to informed stewardship—maximising value, minimising risk, and sustaining wealth across generations.

How to Buy Without Getting Burned

In the pursuit of owning physical gold and silver, the path from intention to possession is fraught with pitfalls that can erode value, trust, and peace of mind. The market's growing accessibility, powered by online platforms and global dealers, offers unprecedented opportunities but simultaneously opens the door to fraud, inflated premiums, and ill-advised purchases. Navigating this terrain safely demands more than casual research—it requires a disciplined approach grounded in trust, transparency, and rigorous due diligence. This article provides a comprehensive guide to acquiring precious metals with confidence, minimising risk, and maximising long-term security.

The first principle in buying precious metals is recognising that *trust is the currency of the transaction.* Unlike stocks or bonds, which are registered electronically, physical metals are tangible assets whose authenticity and provenance must be established unequivocally. Reputable dealers are not merely sales outlets; they are custodians of trust, offering verified products, clear documentation, and transparent pricing. Choosing dealers with a proven track record, robust regulatory compliance, and membership in recognised industry associations—such as the London Bullion Market Association (LBMA) or the Professional Numismatists Guild (PNG)—significantly mitigates risks. These organisations enforce standards that promote quality assurance and ethical conduct, forming an essential first line of defence against deception.

In recent years, *online platforms* have revolutionised metals acquisition by broadening access and improving price transparency. However, they demand heightened vigilance. While many online dealers provide secure transactions, verified inventory, and comprehensive customer service, the digital realm also hosts fraudulent operators exploiting anonymity. Investors must scrutinise website security protocols, verify business licenses, and examine customer reviews from independent sources. Platforms that offer transparent pricing models—clearly delineating spot price, premiums, and additional fees—demonstrate a commitment to honesty. Moreover, secure payment methods, such as bank transfers or escrow services, enhance protection against scams. Caution is warranted when encountering offers that seem too good to be true, especially in unregulated marketplaces or through peer-to-peer channels.

Auctions present another avenue for metals acquisition, offering the potential for competitive pricing and access to rare or collectible items. However, auctions carry unique risks, including overbidding driven by emotional impulses and the purchase of items with uncertain provenance or condition. Success in auctions requires familiarity with the grading and certification standards of precious metals, alongside prudent bidding strategies. Importantly, auctions may include buyer's premiums and other fees that elevate total cost. Investors interested in auctions should prioritise reputable auction houses specialising in precious metals and ensure thorough due diligence before participation.

Verification of *authenticity and purity* remains paramount regardless of acquisition method. Reliable dealers provide assay certificates and employ secure packaging techniques that guarantee metal content. Familiarity with hallmarking standards—such as those mandated by national mints or international regulatory bodies—equips investors to identify genuine products. Technological tools, including X-ray fluorescence (XRF) analyzers, offer on-the-spot verification but require expertise to interpret. For high-value transactions, independent third-party grading and certification services provide an additional layer of assurance, enhancing resale value and market confidence.

Pricing transparency is equally critical. Investors must understand the components of the total purchase price: spot metal price, premiums, taxes, shipping, and insurance. Premiums fluctuate based on demand, product type, and dealer margins. Being conversant with typical premium ranges for various metals and forms enables recognition of outliers and potential overcharges. Timing purchases during periods of lower demand or promotional offers can reduce premiums, though not at the expense of due diligence. Avoiding impulse purchases motivated by market hype protects against paying inflated prices.

Storage and delivery options also influence buying decisions and risk profiles. Some dealers offer direct shipping to buyers, necessitating secure home storage arrangements. Others provide access to insured vault storage facilities, including segregated or allocated accounts, which may incur fees but reduce theft and loss risks. Understanding these logistics and their cost implications informs a comprehensive assessment of the true cost of ownership. Combining physical possession with secure, professional storage can balance accessibility with safety.

Customer service and post-sale support constitute often-overlooked criteria in selecting a purchasing avenue. Reputable dealers provide clear communication channels, transparent policies for returns and buybacks, and educational resources that empower investors. Responsive support fosters trust and facilitates problem resolution, crucial in a market where transactions involve significant sums and physical assets. Engaging with dealers who prioritise client education and transparency elevates the entire investment experience.

Investors must also remain mindful of *regulatory compliance and tax implications*. Legal frameworks governing the purchase, ownership, and sale of precious metals vary across jurisdictions, affecting documentation, reporting, and potential liabilities. Working with dealers knowledgeable about local regulations ensures adherence and reduces exposure to legal or fiscal complications. Proactive consultation with financial or legal advisors complements dealer guidance and integrates metals acquisition into broader financial planning.

The *human element* remains central to safe metals acquisition. Stories abound of investors misled by slick marketing, counterfeit products, or unscrupulous sellers. These cautionary tales underscore the necessity of patience, skepticism, and continuous learning. Building relationships with trusted professionals, participating in reputable industry forums, and verifying information through multiple sources strengthen resilience against deception. Ultimately, informed vigilance is the investor's best safeguard.

In navigating the multifaceted avenues for acquiring precious metals—dealers, online platforms, auctions—the guiding principle is to prioritise *trust and transparency* above convenience or apparent bargains. Each method offers advantages and challenges, but all demand rigorous scrutiny and due diligence. By approaching metals purchasing with disciplined preparation, clear criteria, and ethical awareness, investors transform a potentially hazardous process into a secure foundation for enduring wealth.

This knowledge empowers readers to approach metals acquisition not as a transactional gamble but as a deliberate, informed act of financial stewardship. It instils confidence to discern reputable sources, evaluate offers critically, and integrate metals ownership safely within a diversified portfolio. Buying without getting burned is not merely about avoiding loss; it is about securing value, trust, and peace of mind—essential ingredients in the stewardship of precious metals as real, enduring wealth.

Stories from the Vault

The experience of owning physical gold and silver transcends charts and market analyses—it unfolds through real lives marked by trust, timing, and sometimes, hard lessons. In this subchapter, we delve into a series of candid anecdotes that reveal the multifaceted realities of metals ownership. These stories illuminate not only the rewards but also the pitfalls that accompany holding tangible wealth, offering readers nuanced perspectives grounded in lived experience. By engaging with these narratives, investors gain invaluable insights into the practical and emotional dimensions of securing, storing, and sometimes losing precious metals.

Consider the case of Eleanor, a retiree who began accumulating gold coins in the early 2000s. Her initial purchases were modest but deliberate, motivated by a desire to preserve wealth beyond volatile equities. Eleanor chose widely recognised sovereign coins and stored them in a secure home safe. For years, her metals quietly retained value, but it was during the 2008 financial crisis that she experienced a profound lesson in timing. Watching stock markets plummet, she resisted the urge to liquidate her metals prematurely, understanding their role as a long-term haven. Years later, when gold prices soared, Eleanor's patient approach was rewarded handsomely. Her story underscores the virtue of *discipline* and *strategic patience* in metals investing—reminding readers that timing is not about frantic market entry and exit but about aligning holdings with one's overarching financial horizon.

In contrast, James's experience offers a cautionary tale about trust and due diligence. Enthralled by a seemingly lucrative online offer, James purchased a sizeable quantity of silver rounds from an unverified seller operating on a lesser-known platform. The initial transaction felt smooth and promising until independent verification revealed inconsistencies in purity marks and weight. Attempts to return the metals were met with resistance, and James ultimately suffered a substantial financial loss. This episode starkly illustrates the *risks inherent in online markets* and the critical importance of verifying dealer credentials, product authenticity, and return policies before committing funds. James's misstep serves as a warning against complacency and the allure of "too good to be true" deals, reinforcing the necessity of *vigilance* and *transparency*.

Storage also emerges as a pivotal theme through the experience of Helena and her family. Following a geopolitical crisis that disrupted banking systems in their home country, Helena's family found themselves unable to access their bank accounts for months.

Fortunately, a portion of their wealth was held in gold bars stored in an offshore vault, which remained accessible and secure. However, their story also reveals the *complexities of storage logistics*: navigating legal jurisdictions, insurance arrangements, and withdrawal protocols demanded patience and careful planning. Their case highlights that secure storage is not simply about placing metals in a safe but about *integrated risk management* that considers political, legal, and operational factors. It also affirms the strategic value of geographical diversification and professional vault services.

Conversely, Michael's story exposes the perils of inadequate storage security. Opting to keep his gold and silver at home to maintain direct control, Michael neglected to invest in proper safes or insurance. When a burglary occurred, he lost a significant portion of his holdings—an emotional and financial blow compounded by the difficulty of proving ownership. This narrative exemplifies the *emotional weight* and practical consequences of storage decisions. It challenges the notion that home storage is inherently preferable and underscores the importance of assessing personal risk tolerance, local security conditions, and the trade-offs between convenience and safety.

Timing the market also features prominently in these lived accounts. Sarah, a professional investor, shares how her early metals purchases coincided with peak market prices driven by speculative fervour. She admits to panic selling during a subsequent price decline, only to re-enter the market years later after thorough research and a recalibrated strategy. Sarah's journey from emotional trading to informed patience epitomises the challenges of managing metals as both financial and psychological assets. Her experience advocates for *education*, *emotional discipline*, and *strategic frameworks* over impulsive reactions.

These stories collectively reveal the *human dimension* of metals ownership, where practical decisions intertwine with trust—both in oneself and in others. The relationship between investor and metal is not static but evolves with shifting markets, geopolitical developments, and personal circumstances. Each narrative provides a distinct lesson: Eleanor teaches endurance; James cautions against haste; Helena exemplifies strategic storage; Michael warns of complacency; Sarah highlights emotional maturity. Together, they construct a mosaic of metals ownership that is as rich in insight as it is varied in experience.

Importantly, these accounts also illustrate that metals investing is not a solitary endeavour. Trusted advisors, reputable dealers, secure storage providers, and informed peer networks form an ecosystem that supports successful ownership. Navigating this ecosystem requires intentional engagement and critical judgment, informed by the experiences of those who have walked the path before. The stories from the vault thus serve as both guidance and inspiration—inviting readers to approach metals ownership not as a transactional abstraction but as a lived, purposeful practice grounded in knowledge and vigilance.

This narrative approach complements the analytical and technical discussions in preceding chapters, grounding theory in reality and statistics in personal context. It reminds investors that behind every bar and coin lies a story—of risk managed, trust earned or broken, fortunes preserved or lost. These stories enrich the intellectual understanding of precious metals by revealing their tangible impact on real lives, cultivating empathy alongside expertise.

In absorbing these lessons, readers gain more than anecdotal interest; they acquire a framework for anticipating challenges, mitigating risks, and embracing metals ownership with both eyes open. Stories from the vault transform metals investing from a distant concept into an accessible, human-centred endeavour—one that rewards preparation, patience, and prudent action. Through these narratives, the abstract notion of "holding gold" becomes a vivid, meaningful reality, imparting wisdom that no chart or textbook alone can convey.

Chapter 5
Digital Gold and the Mirage of Convenience

The appeal of digital gold is immediate and seductive: the ability to acquire precious metals with a few taps, from anywhere in the world, seemingly erasing the traditional barriers of storage, transport, and verification. Over recent years, a sprawling ecosystem of crypto-backed tokens, gold ETFs, and mobile platforms has reshaped access to gold, challenging centuries-old assumptions about ownership and value. Yet, beneath this surface of convenience lies a complex terrain, rife with questions about what it truly means to "own" gold in an increasingly virtual age. This chapter examines both the promise and the pitfalls of digital gold, weighing speed against substance, transparency against trust, and virtual exposure against tangible reality.

Central to the discussion is the rise of tokenised gold products—digital assets purportedly backed by physical metal held in vaults somewhere across the globe. Such innovations have democratised entry to the gold market, enabling small investors to participate without ever handling bars or coins. But this convenience carries subtle risks. Unlike holding bullion directly, digital gold generally requires reliance on custodians or counterparties who control the underlying asset. The invisible chain linking token to metal is vulnerable to failure—fraud, insolvency, mismanagement, or shifting regulations can undermine even the most sophisticated platforms. Investors are therefore compelled to scrutinise not only the technology but also the governance, auditing procedures, and legal frameworks that underpin these offerings.

Understanding the distinction between custodians and counterparties sharpens this tension. Custodians maintain physical assets in segregated accounts, ideally with clear, auditable proof of holdings. Counterparties, by contrast, may provide exposure through synthetic instruments or derivatives, without guaranteeing a one-to-one backing. This difference is crucial: custodial arrangements approximate ownership, whereas derivative claims carry counterparty risk. Recognising this nuance challenges the often-repeated marketing assertion that digital gold is equivalent to physical bullion, demanding due diligence and a measure of scepticism from prudent investors.

Moreover, the very convenience that makes digital gold attractive can, paradoxically, introduce vulnerability. In periods of market turbulence or systemic crisis—when gold's protective qualities are most valuable—digital access may falter due to platform outages, regulatory freezes, or liquidity constraints. Physical metals, by contrast, can be held entirely outside the financial system, offering an insulation that digital holdings cannot. The trade-off between accessibility and control thus becomes a central consideration for modern investors.

Many navigate this dilemma through hybrid strategies, blending digital and physical holdings to balance liquidity, flexibility, and security. Digital gold allows rapid response to market movements, while physical metals provide an unassailable store of value, free from counterparty exposure. Such a strategy reflects a pragmatic reading of the contemporary financial landscape, acknowledging that neither form alone fully addresses the uncertainties of a rapidly evolving market. Blended portfolios encourage investors to calibrate exposure in line with risk tolerance, investment horizon, and confidence in custodial arrangements.

The phenomenon of digital gold also invites reflection on broader philosophical and economic themes. The tension between tangible reality and virtual abstraction mirrors societal shifts towards digitisation, decentralisation, and redefined trust. Gold's ancient role as a concrete anchor of wealth stands in contrast to the digital era's emphasis on intangibility and rapid exchange. Engaging critically with digital gold thus demands a careful balance: embracing innovation without losing sight of the metals' enduring essence.

Illustrative examples bring these considerations into focus. Platforms such as Paxos and Tether Gold offer tokenised products backed by vault holdings, yet questions around transparency and audit frequency persist. Gold ETFs, including SPDR Gold Shares, provide liquid, regulated exposure, yet individual investors rarely hold physical metal. High-profile failures and regulatory interventions serve as cautionary tales, underscoring the hazards of relying solely on digital forms. These examples encourage a reasoned, evidence-based approach that transcends promotional narratives.

Ultimately, understanding digital gold requires moving beyond simplistic dichotomies of "real" versus "virtual." It calls for appreciation of layered ownership structures, governance challenges, and strategic trade-offs. This chapter equips readers with the conceptual tools to assess digital metals critically, to discern where convenience masks fragility, and to design resilient portfolios that integrate both innovation and security. Digital gold is neither panacea nor peril in isolation; it is a transformative development that demands informed, thoughtful engagement. By unpacking its complexities, this chapter empowers investors to navigate the mirage of convenience with discernment, maintaining the book's broader objective: reclaiming clarity, permanence, and dignity in an increasingly abstract financial world.

The Rise of Tokenized Gold: Real Metal or Virtual Hope?

The advent of tokenized gold has introduced a profound shift in how investors interact with one of humanity's oldest stores of value. No longer confined to vaults, coins, or bullion bars, gold—and to a lesser extent silver—can now be owned, traded, and transferred digitally through blockchain tokens, exchange-traded funds (ETFs), and mobile applications. This innovation promises unparalleled convenience and accessibility, but it also poses fundamental questions: Is digital gold truly equivalent to holding physical metal? What is gained—and what is lost—when ownership becomes virtual? Understanding these tensions is essential for any serious investor seeking to integrate precious metals into modern portfolios.

Tokenized gold typically refers to digital assets that represent a claim on physical gold held in custody. Each token corresponds to a fractional ownership of a tangible quantity of metal, theoretically backed one-to-one by bars stored in secure vaults. Proponents argue that tokenization democratizes access, lowering entry barriers through fractionalisation, reducing transaction costs, and enabling instantaneous global transfers without the logistical burdens of physical handling. Platforms such as Paxos Gold, Tether Gold, and Perth Mint Gold Token exemplify this new frontier, leveraging blockchain's transparency and security features to appeal to a tech-savvy, digitally native generation.

Exchange-Traded Funds (ETFs), while not blockchain-based tokens, share many characteristics with tokenized gold. ETFs offer regulated, liquid exposure to gold prices, often holding physical metal in custodial vaults but trading on stock exchanges like shares. Their widespread adoption since the early 2000s has revolutionized gold investing by combining ease of access with institutional oversight. However, ETFs have faced criticism for issues related to redemption limits, creation units, and the disconnection between fund shares and physical delivery rights, highlighting the nuanced distinction between paper claims and outright ownership.

Despite these advancements, digital gold confronts inherent limitations rooted in the nature of ownership and risk. Physical gold confers unmediated possession—a tangible asset that can be held, concealed, and controlled independently of financial institutions or technological infrastructures. Digital gold ownership, by contrast, is mediated through custodians and platforms, introducing *counterparty risk*: the possibility that the issuer or custodian may fail, default, or act fraudulently. History offers sobering examples, from Ponzi schemes masquerading as gold-backed tokens to operational failures within custodial institutions. Even when fully backed, verifying that custodians hold adequate reserves and that audits are rigorous and transparent remains a persistent challenge.

Another critical distinction lies in *liquidity and market mechanics*. Tokenized gold and ETFs provide unprecedented liquidity, enabling rapid buying and selling without physical transport or assay delays. This advantage suits traders and investors prioritising flexibility and immediacy. However, this very liquidity can become illusory during systemic crises or market stress, when redemption requests may be delayed or suspended, and tokens may trade at discounts disconnected from underlying metal prices. Physical gold, while less liquid and requiring storage logistics, offers intrinsic resilience by existing outside digital or institutional infrastructures vulnerable to disruption.

The purported transparency of blockchain, often touted as a panacea, warrants nuanced examination. While blockchain can record token ownership and transfer histories immutably, it does not guarantee custody or physical backing. Investors must scrutinise governance models, third-party audits, and legal frameworks underpinning token issuers. The opacity of some platforms' operations and regulatory ambiguity in various jurisdictions complicate trust assessments. In contrast, physical gold's authenticity is verifiable through established assay marks, certifications, and direct inspection—tangible proofs difficult to replicate or counterfeit.

The rise of digital gold also intersects with broader philosophical and behavioural considerations. Gold's enduring value historically derives not only from physical properties but from deep-seated human trust in its permanence and sovereignty. The abstraction of gold into digital tokens challenges traditional notions of *ownership* and *security*, inviting investors to recalibrate their relationship with money, control, and risk. Some view tokenized gold as a natural evolution—leveraging technology to modernise access—while others regard it as a compromise, trading substance for convenience and exposing owners to new vulnerabilities.

Hybrid investment approaches are emerging in response to these complexities. Many investors allocate to both physical metals and tokenized or ETF exposures, seeking to balance the benefits of liquidity and flexibility with the security of tangible possession. This blended strategy acknowledges that digital gold is neither a perfect substitute nor a mere gimmick but a complementary tool within a diversified portfolio. Such pragmatism reflects a mature understanding that modern wealth management involves layered exposures tailored to individual risk tolerances, time horizons, and trust in counterparties.

Real-world cases illustrate these dynamics vividly. The temporary suspension of redemptions in certain gold ETFs during volatile market periods highlights the fragility embedded in paper ownership. Conversely, token platforms with robust governance and transparent audits have successfully facilitated fractional ownership to investors previously excluded by high entry costs. Yet, scandals involving unbacked or misrepresented tokens serve as cautionary tales, reinforcing the imperative for rigorous scrutiny and scepticism. These examples underscore that digital gold's promise is contingent upon operational integrity, regulatory clarity, and informed investor engagement.

Ultimately, the rise of tokenized gold compels investors to confront foundational questions about value, ownership, and trust in an increasingly digital world. It challenges conventional wisdom while opening new possibilities—presenting opportunities inseparable from risks. This chapter equips readers with frameworks to evaluate tokenized gold critically, distinguishing genuine innovation from virtual hope. It encourages a balanced, evidence-based approach that respects gold's timeless essence even as it embraces contemporary forms.

By understanding what is gained and lost in digitizing gold, investors reclaim agency amid financial transformation. They learn to harness technology without surrendering control, to appreciate convenience without compromising substance, and to construct portfolios that reflect both the realities of modern finance and the enduring qualities of precious metals. The narrative of tokenized gold is still unfolding—but armed with insight and discernment, investors can navigate it with clarity and confidence.

Custodians or Counterparties? Trust in the Invisible Chain

The promise of digital gold—owning precious metals with the convenience of a smartphone app or a blockchain token—has captivated investors worldwide. Yet beneath this promise lies a fundamental and often overlooked question: *Do you truly own the metal, or merely a claim subject to the whims of others?* The distinction between holding metals through custodians and relying on counterparties is not just semantic; it defines the nature of ownership, risk, and trust in a system where physical possession is replaced by invisible chains of promise. Understanding this difference is essential for anyone engaging with digital metals in today's complex financial landscape.

At its core, the question revolves around the legal and practical realities of ownership. When an investor purchases physical gold or silver outright, ownership is tangible and singular: the metal is theirs, stored securely or in their possession, and free from intermediary claims. Digital metals, however, frequently operate within frameworks where the investor's rights are contingent on the custodians or counterparties who hold the physical asset or guarantee exposure. Custodianship involves a trusted third party holding metal in segregated accounts, ostensibly on behalf of the investor. Counterparty arrangements, by contrast, resemble contractual promises to pay the value of metals, often without direct physical backing. This subtle but critical difference frames the *invisible chain* of trust underpinning digital gold and silver.

Custodianship offers an appealing middle ground. Investors retain ownership claims to specific quantities of physical metal, while benefiting from professional storage, insurance, and auditing. Established custodians—such as regulated vault operators or reputable banks—maintain segregated holdings to ensure that investors' assets are not commingled with the custodian's own property. Regular, independent audits verify metal quantities and condition, reinforcing transparency and trust. This model attempts to replicate the security of direct possession within an institutional framework, offering liquidity and operational ease without surrendering fundamental ownership rights. However, the effectiveness of this model depends heavily on custodian integrity, regulatory oversight, and audit rigor—variables that vary across jurisdictions and providers.

Counterparty risk, conversely, lies at the heart of many digital gold products that function as claims rather than direct ownership. Examples include certain exchange-traded notes (ETNs), synthetic gold-backed tokens, or derivative contracts. Investors in these instruments effectively hold promises—agreements contingent on the issuer's solvency and willingness to honour obligations. In stable market conditions, this may seem benign, but history reveals the vulnerability of such arrangements during crises. The collapse of counterparties can render investors unsecured creditors, with minimal recourse to recover value. The 2008 financial crisis offers stark examples where overreliance on counterparty claims led to substantial losses, illustrating that *paper ownership is not equivalent to holding metal.*

Evaluating the trustworthiness of custodians and counterparties requires scrutiny beyond marketing claims. Critical factors include legal ownership structures, jurisdictional protections, insolvency protocols, and transparency of holdings. Investors must assess whether custodians operate under robust regulatory regimes, whether holdings are truly segregated, and if regular, third-party audits are publicly accessible. Similarly, counterparty arrangements warrant careful examination of creditworthiness, collateralisation, and contractual terms defining redemption rights. The *opacity* of some digital gold platforms, especially emerging blockchain-based tokens, compounds these challenges, necessitating heightened due diligence and scepticism.

This invisible chain of trust is further complicated by the evolving regulatory landscape. Jurisdictions vary in how they recognise ownership claims, regulate custodians, and protect investors. Some digital gold products fall into regulatory grey zones, lacking clear classification as securities, commodities, or property. This ambiguity exposes investors to legal uncertainty and potential enforcement gaps. Regulatory developments, while aimed at enhancing transparency and investor protection, can also disrupt market access or complicate redemption processes. Staying informed of these dynamics is crucial for maintaining trust and anticipating risks.

Technological innovations such as blockchain promise to enhance transparency and reduce counterparty risk by providing immutable ownership records and automating contractual enforcement through smart contracts. Yet, blockchain's transparency addresses only part of the trust equation; it cannot guarantee the existence or quality of the underlying physical metal. The "oracle problem"—the challenge of reliably linking real-world assets to digital records—remains unresolved. Thus, blockchain's role is to complement, not replace, traditional custodianship and verification mechanisms.

The human dimension of trust cannot be overstated. Trust is not merely an abstract concept but a living contract between investor and institution, shaped by reputation, history, and behaviour. Investors must cultivate relationships with providers, seek transparent communication, and verify claims independently. This proactive engagement transforms trust from blind faith into informed confidence, reducing vulnerability to fraud or operational failure.

Case studies exemplify these issues. The high-profile collapse of a tokenized gold platform due to mismanagement left investors scrambling for recovery, highlighting risks in nascent digital metals ecosystems. Conversely, well-established custodial services with transparent audits have maintained investor confidence through volatile markets, demonstrating the resilience possible when trust is institutionalised. These contrasting outcomes underscore that trust in digital metals is neither automatic nor uniform; it is earned, maintained, and sometimes broken.

For investors, recognising whether they hold metals through custodianship or mere counterparty claims informs risk management and portfolio strategy. Those valuing absolute control may prioritise physical ownership or custodial arrangements with strong legal protections. Others seeking liquidity and ease might accept counterparty exposures, balancing convenience against risk. This clarity enables purpose-driven investing rather than reliance on ambiguous promises.

In a financial environment increasingly defined by digital innovation and abstract assets, the *invisible chain* of trust binding investors to digital metals demands careful navigation. Understanding the distinctions between custodians and counterparties, evaluating governance and legal safeguards, and maintaining critical awareness equips investors to engage with digital gold and silver intelligently. This vigilance preserves the essence of metals ownership—real value secured in an uncertain world—even as its form adapts to the possibilities and perils of the digital age.

When Speed Betrays Substance

In a world increasingly enamoured with immediacy, the appeal of digital platforms for purchasing and managing gold and silver is undeniable. The convenience of instant transactions, real-time pricing, and mobile access has transformed the metals market into a 24/7 arena. Yet, this acceleration of access and control carries hidden vulnerabilities, particularly when speed eclipses substance. The ease of clicking "buy" on a digital gold platform masks crucial fragilities in ownership, custody, and resilience—fragilities that can become starkly apparent in moments of crisis. For investors seeking to preserve wealth, recognising when convenience undermines security is not merely prudent but essential.

The allure of digital metals platforms is built on the promise of frictionless experience: no vault visits, no physical handling, no complex logistics. Fractional ownership through tokens or accounts allows entry with minimal capital, and the instantaneous nature of transfers enables nimble portfolio adjustments. This immediacy resonates with contemporary expectations shaped by fintech innovations across finance. Yet, this very convenience often abstracts away the physical realities and legal protections that underpin traditional metals ownership. When digital systems fail—due to technical outages, regulatory intervention, or cyberattacks—the investor's access to assets can vanish or become severely restricted, revealing that *speed is only valuable if underpinned by robustness*.

Historical episodes illuminate the dangers of overreliance on digital platforms. During the financial turmoil of March 2020, when markets experienced extreme volatility triggered by the COVID-19 pandemic, many investors discovered that certain gold-backed ETFs and token platforms temporarily halted redemptions or suffered liquidity constraints. These interruptions occurred precisely when the safe-haven qualities of gold were most sought after. Similarly, reports of cyber breaches targeting digital asset custodians highlight that no online platform is impervious to disruption. Unlike physical bullion that can be stored independently or geographically diversified, digital holdings remain tethered to the operational integrity and solvency of third-party providers. This dependency *introduces a layer of systemic risk* not immediately visible in the promise of instant transactions.

Technical infrastructure also plays a critical role in determining resilience. Digital gold platforms depend on complex software ecosystems, blockchain networks, and internet connectivity. Each layer presents potential failure points. Distributed denial-of-service (DDoS) attacks, software bugs, or hardware malfunctions can render platforms inaccessible or compromise transaction integrity. For investors, these technological risks translate into uncertainty: can they liquidate when needed? Are their holdings accurately represented? The potential for *"black swan"* events—rare but devastating failures—must be accounted for in any assessment of digital metals' reliability.

The regulatory environment compounds these challenges. Digital gold platforms often operate in fragmented jurisdictions, with varying degrees of oversight. Regulatory crackdowns or sudden policy shifts can impose freezes on trading, restrict withdrawals, or reclassify assets, affecting investor access and value. The opacity and novelty of some platforms amplify regulatory risk, creating environments where legal recourse is uncertain. Physical metals, by contrast, are tangible assets with well-established legal frameworks supporting ownership rights. This contrast highlights that *regulatory resilience is as important as technological convenience.*

Psychological factors influence investor behaviour in the context of digital metals. The ease of online transactions may encourage reactive trading, driven by market noise rather than strategic planning. The "buy and forget" mentality suited to physical bullion ownership can be eroded by the temptation of constant portfolio tinkering. This behavioural shift risks commoditising precious metals, detracting from their traditional role as long-term stores of value and strategic hedges. The illusion of control afforded by digital platforms can lead to *overconfidence*, while masking the underlying fragility of digital custody.

Mitigating these vulnerabilities requires a conscious approach that values *resilience over rapidity*. Diversifying holdings between digital and physical forms enhances portfolio robustness. Physical metals held in secure, insured vaults provide a tangible fallback when digital systems falter. Conversely, digital gold can supplement physical holdings by offering liquidity and trading flexibility in stable market conditions. This blended strategy acknowledges the complementary strengths and weaknesses of each form, allowing investors to leverage convenience without sacrificing security.

Education and due diligence underpin effective resilience. Investors must scrutinise platform governance, custody arrangements, audit transparency, and user protections. Understanding the contractual terms defining redemption rights and counterparty obligations is vital. Moreover, preparing for contingencies—including technical failures or market disruptions—through diversified storage and exit planning transforms potential vulnerabilities into managed risks.

The philosophical tension between *speed and substance* embodied by digital metals reflects broader societal trade-offs in a digitised economy. Convenience, while seductive, often entails hidden costs. Metals investors anchored in the enduring qualities of precious metals must resist the allure of instant gratification when it undermines the fundamental purpose of ownership: security, sovereignty, and stability. This discerning stance aligns with a wider investment ethos valuing *patience, prudence, and preparedness.*

Ultimately, recognising when speed betrays substance equips investors to navigate the digital metals landscape judiciously. It fosters a mindset that appreciates technological advances while respecting the immutable principles that have sustained precious metals' value for millennia. This balance safeguards wealth—not only in normal times but, critically, in the crises that test the true resilience of all assets.

Blended Strategies: Combining Digital and Physical for Modern Resilience

The evolving landscape of precious metals investment challenges traditional paradigms, inviting a re-examination of how best to harness gold and silver's enduring value in a digital age. The polarisation between physical ownership and digital access has often been cast as a binary choice—tangible bars in vaults versus instantaneous tokenised holdings. Yet, for the discerning investor, this dichotomy is a false one. A *blended strategy* that thoughtfully combines physical metals with digital exposures offers a nuanced path toward resilience, balancing liquidity, accessibility, and security in a manner aligned with contemporary financial realities.

At its essence, a blended approach recognises that physical gold and silver possess irreplaceable attributes: they are sovereign assets, immune to cyber risks, and physically verifiable. Holding bullion or sovereign coins in secure, insured vaults or trusted home safes provides an unassailable store of value, free from counterparty obligations. This *tangible permanence* forms the bedrock of wealth preservation, especially during systemic shocks that disrupt electronic markets or undermine trust in intermediaries. However, physical metals face limitations in liquidity and transaction speed. Selling or transferring physical metal can be cumbersome, costly, and slow—particularly in times of market stress when immediacy is critical.

Digital gold, encompassing tokenised metals, exchange-traded funds (ETFs), and app-based holdings, addresses this very constraint by offering near-instant access to market pricing and ease of transaction. Investors can adjust positions swiftly, engage in fractional ownership, and seamlessly integrate metals exposure into diversified portfolios alongside stocks, bonds, and cryptocurrencies. This *digital agility* complements the physical asset's steadfastness, creating a dynamic balance between readiness and reliability. Yet digital metals carry inherent vulnerabilities: reliance on custodians or counterparties, technological risks, regulatory uncertainties, and potential disconnects from actual physical reserves.

The optimal blend depends on the investor's objectives, risk tolerance, and investment horizon. For instance, a pragmatic portfolio might allocate a substantial core holding to physical metals—safeguarded in geographically diversified vaults with strong audit trails—to ensure enduring security and sovereignty. Simultaneously, a portion of metals exposure could reside in tokenised gold or ETFs, enabling swift reallocation, liquidity during emergencies, or participation in speculative opportunities without the logistical overhead of physical handling. This stratification mitigates the risks of any single mode of ownership, enhancing overall resilience.

The implementation of blended strategies requires discerning evaluation of providers and products. Physical holdings demand attention to purity, provenance, storage security, and insurance. Choosing recognised mints, accredited vault operators, and insured custodians is vital. Digital assets necessitate scrutiny of platform governance, audit transparency, legal frameworks, and counterparty risk. Investors should prioritise platforms that offer clear redemption mechanisms and verifiable metal backing. Balancing these considerations ensures that neither convenience nor security is sacrificed unduly.

Case studies illuminate the practical benefits of hybrid approaches. During periods of market turbulence, investors with exclusive reliance on digital metals sometimes faced withdrawal delays or platform outages. Those maintaining physical reserves could draw on tangible assets as anchors, reducing forced sales at depressed prices. Conversely, investors holding solely physical metals sometimes struggled with illiquidity when rapid portfolio adjustments were necessary. Those combining forms navigated both extremes more effectively, demonstrating that blending optimises response agility without compromising asset permanence.

Blended strategies also respond to behavioural dimensions of investing. Digital metals cater to modern preferences for immediacy, transparency, and fractionalisation, appealing to younger or more tech-oriented demographics. Physical metals resonate with traditional values of sovereignty, tangibility, and trust accumulated over centuries. Integrating both addresses diverse investor psychologies, fostering balanced portfolios that align with evolving expectations without forsaking foundational principles.

Furthermore, blended ownership reflects an adaptive mindset essential in a financial ecosystem characterised by rapid innovation and persistent uncertainty. It recognises that *no single form of ownership is universally optimal*; rather, resilience emerges from diversification across dimensions of custody, liquidity, and control. This flexibility empowers investors to navigate shifting regulatory landscapes, technological disruptions, and geopolitical risks with greater confidence.

The ethical dimension of metals ownership gains nuance through blending. Investors concerned with responsible sourcing and environmental impact can leverage certified physical products alongside digital instruments with transparent audit trails. This combination supports values-driven investing while maintaining practical functionality.

In practice, constructing a blended metals portfolio involves ongoing calibration. Market conditions, personal circumstances, and technological developments necessitate periodic reassessment of allocations between physical and digital holdings. Effective stewardship involves not only initial selection but dynamic management—balancing security, cost, convenience, and risk as contexts evolve.

Ultimately, blending digital and physical precious metals represents a *sophisticated evolution* in metals investing, marrying ancient principles with modern realities. It transcends simplistic binaries, offering a pathway that honours the enduring essence of metals as stores of value while embracing the benefits of contemporary innovation. This hybrid strategy equips investors to preserve wealth and seize opportunity in a complex, interconnected world—achieving resilience not through rigidity but through informed, flexible integration.

By adopting blended approaches, investors reclaim agency over their metals exposure—combining the best of both worlds to build portfolios that are not only secure and durable but also responsive and efficient. This strategy embodies the forward-thinking ethos necessary for metals ownership in the 21st century, translating historical wisdom into practical, actionable frameworks for enduring financial sovereignty.

Chapter 6
Storage as Strategy

Owning gold and silver is only part of the story; the other, equally crucial aspect is determining where and how to store these metals—a decision that blends practical security with deeper questions of sovereignty, trust, and control. The act of physical custody transforms abstract wealth into something palpably real, yet it also introduces a web of logistical, emotional, and even geopolitical considerations that shape an investor's relationship with their assets. This chapter examines storage not simply as a technical obligation but as a strategic dimension of ownership, where the balance between safety, accessibility, and agency comes into sharp relief.

The first crossroads for any metals investor is the choice between keeping holdings at home or entrusting them to professional vaults. Home storage appeals to a fundamental desire for sovereignty—the reassurance of wealth literally in one's hands, shielded from intermediaries, banks, or government intervention. There is undeniable comfort in that immediacy, especially during uncertain times. Yet it comes with tangible challenges: procuring secure safes, arranging insurance, devising concealment strategies, and maintaining constant vigilance against theft or mishap. Vault storage, by contrast, offers high-grade security, insurance coverage, and often geographic diversification, though it trades away the tactile certainty of direct possession. The tension between control and convenience underpins the architecture of metals storage, framing how investors weigh institutional trust against personal agency.

Beyond the local choice lies the more intricate geography of trust that shapes offshore storage decisions. Certain jurisdictions—Switzerland, Singapore, Liechtenstein, among others—have earned reputations for financial discretion, robust legal protections, and political stability. Storing metals abroad requires not only assessing the physical security of vaults but also understanding the legal and regulatory environments that govern asset protection and recovery. Such jurisdictional diversification serves as a hedge against domestic policy changes, capital controls, or geopolitical shocks. Yet it also demands navigating complex tax considerations, cross-border logistics, and access protocols. The geopolitics of storage, therefore, emerges as a critical and often underappreciated facet of metals investment strategy.

Nested within these macro considerations is the art of designing a personal "metal map"—a discreet, secure, and customised plan that aligns with an individual's lifestyle, risk tolerance, and investment objectives. Balancing concealment with accessibility, secrecy with practicality, is key. Some investors divide holdings between home safes, local bank vaults, and offshore facilities, each with distinct security arrangements and retrieval processes. Others incorporate technological enhancements—biometric locks, encrypted inventories, or secure digital tracking—to bolster discretion and control. Crafting such a map requires foresight, discipline, and a nuanced understanding of both personal and systemic risks, turning storage from an afterthought into a deliberate, evolving strategy.

The stakes of these decisions are brought sharply into focus during the ritual of retrieval. Accessing metals can become urgent, complicated, or even impossible in moments of crisis. Accounts abound of investors caught off guard: barred from vaults during political upheavals, unable to move metals across borders due to sudden restrictions, or delayed by bureaucratic bottlenecks. Conversely, stories of those who planned meticulously—establishing retrieval contingencies and redundancies—highlight the benefits of proactive preparation. These experiences underline that storage is not static; it demands regular review, contingency planning, and a readiness to act. The act of retrieval illuminates storage as an active, sometimes existential, component of true ownership.

This chapter encourages readers to reconceive storage as a strategic pillar, one where decisions speak to broader commitments: autonomy, privacy, and resilience. Choices about storage influence liquidity, risk exposure, and the very emotional tenor of ownership, bridging abstract wealth with the tangible permanence of metals. By exploring trade-offs, geographic considerations, and practical logistics, the chapter provides frameworks for robust, adaptable strategies capable of safeguarding value across varied scenarios.

In exposing the layered realities of metals storage, this discussion moves the conversation beyond mere purchase and price. True ownership encompasses not just acquisition but how metals are held, where they reside, and how they can be accessed when most needed. Storage emerges not as a passive necessity but as a vital strategic art—one that, when mastered, fortifies both the permanence and the sovereignty central to precious metals investment.

Where Safety Meets Sovereignty: Home vs Vault

The question of where to store gold and silver—whether nestled securely within the confines of one's home or entrusted to the guarded vaults of third-party institutions—is as much a matter of philosophy as it is logistics. It is a choice that reverberates beyond physical security, touching on profound issues of personal sovereignty, trust, access, and psychological comfort. This decision sits at the intersection of tangible safety and intangible autonomy, shaping not only how metals are preserved but how their owners relate to their wealth. The following exploration unpacks the emotional and practical trade-offs inherent in storing precious metals at home versus placing them in professional vaults, offering readers a foundation to make intentional, informed choices aligned with their values and circumstances.

Storing metals at home conjures a visceral sense of control and immediacy. For many investors, the ability to hold gold coins or bars in hand symbolizes ultimate sovereignty—a direct, unmediated connection to wealth that no external party can sever or withhold. This intimacy with one's assets can provide emotional reassurance amid financial uncertainty, where institutional failures, capital controls, or geopolitical turmoil threaten access to external holdings. Home storage offers immediate liquidity without intermediaries, bypassing concerns over custodian solvency or bureaucratic delays. However, this sovereignty exacts a demanding price: the responsibility of securing metals against theft, fire, natural disasters, and even simple loss falls squarely on the owner. High-quality safes, alarm systems, insurance policies, and discretion become critical layers of defence, each presenting logistical and financial challenges. The psychological burden of constant vigilance can weigh heavily, especially as holding substantial metals at home may invite anxiety over exposure or potential discovery.

By contrast, third-party vaults promise professional-grade security, robust insurance, and institutional safeguards that many private owners cannot replicate. Reputable vault operators employ advanced physical security measures—armed guards, biometric access, redundant alarm systems, and fire suppression—creating environments optimised for preservation and risk mitigation. Such facilities also provide legal structures that segregate client assets, ensuring that metals are not mingled with the vault's property or accessible in cases of insolvency. Entrusting metals to a vault can relieve owners of the operational complexities of home security and facilitate administrative conveniences, such as storage receipts, audits, and streamlined liquidation processes. For high-net-worth individuals and institutional investors, vault storage enables scale and diversification not easily achievable at home.

Yet, vault storage introduces its own set of challenges, chiefly concerning access and trust. Unlike the tangible reassurance of physical possession, vault holdings are inherently indirect. Access may be subject to procedural hurdles, operating hours, withdrawal limits, and, critically, geopolitical or regulatory constraints. Historical precedents demonstrate that, in times of crisis, governments or financial authorities have imposed capital controls, restricted vault withdrawals, or frozen assets, complicating or even obstructing access. For example, during Argentina's 2001 financial collapse, many investors found their overseas vault holdings inaccessible due to regulatory actions. This reality underscores that custody is not synonymous with ownership sovereignty; entrusting metals to third parties involves ceding a degree of control and assuming counterparty risk.

The question of trust thus emerges as pivotal. Home storage presumes self-reliance, requiring the owner to cultivate expertise in security and risk management. Vault storage depends on the reputation, transparency, and resilience of custodial institutions. Investors must evaluate vault providers' credentials, insurance coverage, audit protocols, and regulatory compliance. Jurisdictional factors also bear weight—vaults located in politically stable countries with robust legal protections offer advantages over those in volatile regions. The choice of storage location becomes a strategic decision informed by geopolitical assessments as much as by physical security measures.

Furthermore, the economics of storage merit careful consideration. Home storage entails upfront costs for safes, security systems, and insurance premiums, alongside ongoing maintenance and the potential opportunity cost of immobilised capital. Vault storage typically involves annual fees calculated as a percentage of the metal's value, which can vary widely based on facility, location, and service level. These fees impact overall returns and must be weighed against the security and convenience benefits provided. For modest holdings, vault fees may erode investment value disproportionately, whereas for larger portfolios, professional storage can offer economies of scale.

Another dimension influencing the home versus vault debate is *discretion and confidentiality*. Keeping metals at home allows investors to maintain privacy without sharing information with external parties. Vault storage, while generally confidential, may require disclosures that could become accessible in legal disputes or through regulatory scrutiny. In contexts where financial privacy is paramount, this factor can be decisive. Conversely, home storage carries risks if secrecy is compromised through theft, prying acquaintances, or public exposure.

The nature of one's lifestyle and risk profile also shapes storage preferences. Individuals with frequent travel, unstable residences, or those anticipating relocation may favour vault storage for logistical simplicity and secure continuity. Conversely, those with strong attachment to physical control, or residing in jurisdictions with unstable financial institutions, might prioritise home storage despite its burdens. Some investors combine both approaches, segmenting holdings between home and vault to balance sovereignty, accessibility, and risk diversification.

Real-life experiences illustrate the nuances of this decision. A seasoned investor recounted storing a significant portion of gold at home in a concealed, fortified safe, which provided peace of mind during political unrest when banks imposed withdrawal limits. Another account involved a family who stored metals in a Swiss vault, benefiting from the country's legal protections and political neutrality but facing frustrating delays during vault access amid regulatory changes. These stories reflect that neither option guarantees absolute security or convenience; rather, each involves trade-offs that must be managed thoughtfully.

In evaluating home versus vault storage, it is essential to transcend simplistic binaries and appreciate storage as a continuum where safety and sovereignty intersect. True security encompasses not only physical protection but legal ownership clarity, ease of access, privacy, and adaptability to changing circumstances. Decisions about storage must be integrated with broader portfolio strategies, lifestyle considerations, and risk tolerance, reflecting a holistic understanding of what it means to own precious metals in a complex world.

Ultimately, where safety meets sovereignty is a terrain of personal values and practical realities. Choosing between home and vault storage is not merely a logistical task but a strategic act that shapes the investor's relationship to wealth, control, and risk. By illuminating the emotional and operational dimensions of this choice, this exploration empowers readers to design storage solutions that honour both the physical permanence of metals and the human need for agency and peace of mind.

The Geography of Trust: Offshore Storage and Political Risk

When it comes to safeguarding precious metals, the question of *where* to store is inseparable from the question of *whom* to trust—and trust, in this context, is deeply geographical. Offshore storage has emerged as a crucial strategy for investors seeking to protect assets from domestic instability, capital controls, or regulatory intervention. However, the choice of jurisdiction is far from trivial; it involves navigating a complex web of political, legal, and economic factors that collectively define the contours of trust. Understanding the geography of secure storage—and the political risks embedded within it—is essential for constructing resilient portfolios in an unpredictable world.

Certain countries have long cultivated reputations as safe havens for wealth preservation, offering vault facilities that combine stringent security, robust legal frameworks, and political stability. Switzerland often stands at the forefront of this list. Its decades-old tradition of banking secrecy, political neutrality, and a strong rule of law has translated into a vault infrastructure renowned for discretion and reliability. Swiss vault operators maintain rigorous audit procedures and insured storage options, serving clients worldwide who seek assurance against both physical and geopolitical risks. Yet, Swiss neutrality also comes with complications; increasing international pressure for transparency has led to erosion of banking secrecy, and regulatory tightening may impact confidentiality and access over time. Hence, even this venerable jurisdiction is not immune to shifting political winds.

Singapore represents a newer, but rapidly growing, hub for precious metals storage in Asia. Its strategic location, political stability, and business-friendly environment have attracted investors wary of regional volatility. Singapore's vault operators offer high-tech security and transparent legal ownership structures, while the government's commitment to the rule of law underpins investor confidence. However, the city-state's close economic ties with China and Western powers introduce a delicate balancing act, where geopolitical tensions can influence regulatory developments. Singapore exemplifies how emerging vault jurisdictions blend opportunity with complexity, demanding nuanced risk assessment.

Liechtenstein, Luxembourg, and other smaller European nations have also carved niches as trusted vault locations. Their advantage often lies in niche legal frameworks that permit confidential ownership and offer asset protection against creditors or state interference. These jurisdictions appeal particularly to investors focused on wealth preservation and succession planning. However, smaller nations face their own challenges, such as exposure to broader EU regulations, susceptibility to international sanctions, or economic dependencies that may alter their political calculus. These subtleties underscore that vault security is never absolute but context-dependent.

Beyond well-established financial centres, offshore storage options span diverse locations, from the Cayman Islands to Dubai and beyond. Each jurisdiction brings distinct combinations of legal tradition, regulatory oversight, political risk, and cultural attitudes toward wealth. The choice is not merely one of convenience or cost but a strategic calculation of jurisdictional resilience—the likelihood that storage arrangements will withstand political upheaval, legal challenges, or expropriation. Investors must engage deeply with the *politics of storage*, recognising that vault safety is intertwined with sovereignty, international relations, and domestic governance.

This understanding leads naturally to the concept of *jurisdictional diversification*—the deliberate allocation of metals holdings across multiple geographical locations to mitigate concentrated political risk. Much like financial diversification reduces market risk, spreading physical assets across vaults in different countries shields investors from single points of failure. For example, metals stored exclusively in one country may become inaccessible if that nation imposes capital controls or experiences political unrest. Diversifying across jurisdictions with varied legal traditions and geopolitical alignments increases the probability that at least a portion of holdings remains accessible and protected. However, diversification introduces logistical complexities, increased costs, and heightened administrative burdens, demanding a sophisticated approach that balances risk reduction with operational feasibility.

The nuanced interplay between security and sovereignty is evident when assessing the legal rights of owners in various jurisdictions. While some countries provide explicit statutes safeguarding private ownership and vault confidentiality, others may permit government intervention or legal claims on stored assets. This variability has tangible consequences: the potential for asset freezing, forced disclosure, or prolonged litigation can transform storage from protection into vulnerability. Investors must scrutinise local property laws, judicial independence, and historical precedents to gauge jurisdictional trustworthiness beyond surface reputation.

Recent political developments illustrate the fragility of trust in offshore storage. The tightening of anti-money laundering regulations globally has led to enhanced scrutiny of vault operators and their clients. International cooperation between tax authorities, while beneficial for transparency, risks compromising confidentiality and imposing onerous compliance requirements. In some cases, political shifts have triggered retroactive investigations or seizure of assets, as seen in high-profile cases involving politically exposed persons or sanctioned individuals. These realities confirm that no jurisdiction is entirely insulated from political risk, and *trust must be continuously calibrated* against evolving geopolitical dynamics.

Case studies of geopolitical crises further illuminate the stakes of jurisdictional choice. During the 2014 Crimea crisis, for example, Russian investors holding metals in Ukrainian or neighboring vaults faced uncertainty and difficulty accessing their assets amid sanctions and border restrictions. Similarly, in Venezuela, hyperinflation and government seizures rendered domestic vaults inaccessible or unreliable, forcing many investors to seek offshore alternatives hastily. These episodes underscore that physical security without political stability offers limited protection and that the *geography of trust is dynamic* and context-sensitive.

The role of technology and transparency also influences jurisdictional trust. Countries and vault operators embracing rigorous third-party audits, blockchain-based ownership records, and real-time reporting foster greater investor confidence. Conversely, jurisdictions lacking regulatory clarity or operating in opaque environments amplify risk through uncertainty. Modern investors increasingly demand evidence of *verifiable metal backing* and clear legal ownership, shifting the competitive landscape of vault locations toward those embracing accountability.

Investors must also consider the tax implications tied to jurisdictional choices. Tax treaties, reporting obligations, and inheritance laws vary widely, affecting net returns and estate planning. Some jurisdictions offer favourable tax treatment for stored metals, while others impose levies that can erode wealth preservation goals. Navigating this fiscal terrain requires expert advice and foresight, integrating tax strategy with storage decisions for holistic wealth management.

Ultimately, the geography of trust is not static but a strategic framework demanding ongoing attention. It requires investors to think globally, anticipate political shifts, and diversify thoughtfully—not only across assets but across borders. This mindset transforms metals storage from a passive safeguard into an active dimension of portfolio resilience. The choice of vault jurisdiction encapsulates a profound dialogue between security and sovereignty, certainty and contingency, permanence and flux.

By engaging deeply with the political, legal, and cultural underpinnings of offshore storage, investors reclaim agency over where and how their metals endure. This understanding transcends mere convenience, situating storage decisions within the broader geopolitical architecture shaping the future of wealth. Navigating this landscape with clarity and discernment equips investors to build protective geographies of trust—networks of secure storage poised to withstand the unpredictable tides of global change.

Concealment vs Access: Designing Your Own Metal Map

In the realm of precious metals ownership, the challenge of storage transcends mere security; it is a delicate balancing act between *concealment* and *access*. Investors must navigate the tension between keeping their gold and silver sufficiently discreet to deter theft or unwanted attention, while ensuring that these assets remain readily retrievable when needed. This dual imperative demands a carefully crafted, personalised "metal map" — a strategic layout of storage locations and methods aligned with one's lifestyle, risk tolerance, and financial objectives. Designing this map requires insight, foresight, and an appreciation of the nuanced interplay between secrecy, security, and liquidity.

Concealment serves as the frontline defence against physical threats: burglary, coercion, or intrusion. The instinct to hide precious metals in places unknown to all but a trusted few is ancient and universal. Yet concealment is not simply about secrecy; it is about *effective* secrecy. For instance, hiding gold coins in an obvious safe tucked behind a painting is far less secure than distributing holdings across cleverly disguised, decentralised locations. Investors must consider the profiles of potential adversaries—whether opportunistic thieves, intrusive authorities, or careless acquaintances—and tailor concealment strategies accordingly. This can involve everything from innovative home safes camouflaged as everyday objects, to encrypted records of vault locations, to physical distribution across multiple secure sites.

At the same time, concealment that impedes access can undermine the very purpose of ownership. A metal cache that is so secret it becomes inaccessible in an emergency is effectively worthless. The risk of losing track of keys, forgetting combinations, or suffering health or mobility setbacks necessitates built-in redundancies. Access planning encompasses not only physical retrieval logistics but also legal and administrative preparedness. Investors should ensure that trusted proxies or heirs are informed and authorised to access holdings if the owner is incapacitated. Furthermore, access must be feasible under various scenarios, including travel restrictions, political instability, or natural disasters, which might disrupt usual routes or protocols.

Creating an effective metal map thus involves *distributed risk management.* Concentrating all holdings in one location maximises convenience but magnifies vulnerability; dispersing metals across several locations enhances resilience but complicates oversight and control. Investors must decide how to segment their holdings based on priorities. For example, a core emergency reserve might be kept in a highly secure but less accessible vault, while smaller, liquid caches could be stored closer at hand for immediate needs. International diversification adds another dimension, allowing assets to be positioned in jurisdictions with varying political and legal environments, further insulating against localized disruptions.

The choice of storage types also factors into this design. Private home safes confer autonomy and instant access but require vigilant security measures and insurance. Bank safe deposit boxes offer institutional security but may restrict access hours and are subject to regulatory or operational risks. Professional bullion vaults, often located offshore, provide high levels of security and segregation but involve withdrawal fees, procedural formalities, and potential geopolitical risk. Integrating these options into a cohesive plan demands thorough evaluation of each method's strengths and limitations in relation to the investor's specific needs.

Psychological elements influence metal map design as well. The peace of mind derived from knowing one's metals are safely stored can be undermined by anxieties over potential loss or inaccessibility. Conversely, overly complex storage arrangements may breed confusion or neglect. Striking a balance requires candid self-assessment: How much risk is tolerable? How comfortable is the owner with technological aids, such as encrypted digital logs or biometric locks? How involved do they wish to be in day-to-day management? Answers to these questions shape the contours of the storage strategy.

Real-world examples highlight the critical importance of thoughtful metal map design. During the 2008 financial crisis, some investors with substantial holdings in single vaults faced delays accessing their metals amid regulatory scrutiny and market turmoil. Others who had diversified storage, including discreet home reserves, could draw on immediate liquidity. Similarly, political upheavals in various countries have rendered vault-stored metals inaccessible to owners cut off by travel bans or asset freezes, underscoring the value of jurisdictional and physical dispersion. These experiences illustrate that *storage without strategic planning exposes investors to avoidable risks.*

Technology offers new tools to enhance both concealment and access. Digital vault management platforms provide encrypted inventories and remote monitoring, while blockchain-based ownership certificates add transparency and traceability without compromising privacy. Yet reliance on technology introduces dependencies that must be weighed against physical control. Investors must evaluate cybersecurity risks, backup procedures, and the integrity of digital custodians as integral components of their metal map.

Designing a personal metal map is ultimately an exercise in *intentionality.* It demands a holistic perspective that marries physical realities with psychological needs and contextual risks. Storage choices should not be reactive or ad hoc but founded on clear principles: optimising security, maintaining flexibility, safeguarding confidentiality, and ensuring accessibility under diverse scenarios.

This strategic approach transforms storage from a passive concern into a dynamic, integral facet of metals ownership.

The process also benefits from professional consultation. Security experts, legal advisors, and trusted vault operators can provide critical insights tailored to the investor's profile. Periodic reviews and drills—such as testing access protocols or simulating retrieval under constrained conditions—enhance preparedness and confidence. By engaging proactively with the complexities of concealment and access, investors cultivate a robust framework that supports not only asset preservation but also peace of mind.

In the end, the art of designing one's metal map reflects the broader ethos of precious metals ownership: a commitment to enduring value secured through thoughtful, informed stewardship. It embodies the recognition that wealth protection transcends mere possession; it requires deliberate architecture of where, how, and by whom metals are held and accessed. This mindful strategy empowers investors to navigate uncertainty with greater control, resilience, and assurance.

The Ritual of Retrieval

The act of acquiring gold or silver is only the beginning of a much longer commitment—one that culminates in *retrieval*: the process of accessing your metals when circumstances demand. This ritual, often overlooked in planning, is where theory meets reality, and where well-laid storage strategies are tested under pressure. History and contemporary experience reveal that the ability—or inability—to retrieve precious metals in moments of crisis can make the difference between security and vulnerability, between calm confidence and acute loss. Examining gripping accounts of retrieval underscores the critical importance of foresight, preparation, and adaptability in metals ownership.

One of the most poignant lessons emerges from political crises where vault access became severely constrained or impossible.

Consider the experience of investors during the 2008 financial crisis who held significant amounts of gold in bank vaults within jurisdictions suddenly subject to capital controls and regulatory lockdowns. Several reported lengthy delays or outright denials of access as governments imposed withdrawal limits to preserve financial stability. In some cases, metals were effectively trapped, inaccessible for months or longer despite legal ownership. These episodes demonstrate that legal title alone does not guarantee timely physical control—a sobering reminder that retrieval is as much a function of the political environment as of storage location.

Equally instructive are stories of private owners who placed trust in home safes without comprehensive contingency plans. One case involved an elderly couple who kept a sizeable gold collection concealed in a home safe but failed to share access information or keys with trusted family members. Following a medical emergency that rendered them incapacitated, their heirs faced bureaucratic hurdles and uncertainty about the metals' whereabouts and legitimacy, delaying access during a period of financial vulnerability. This scenario highlights the human and procedural dimensions of retrieval: it is not enough to have metals securely stored; owners must ensure clear, legally sound instructions and practical mechanisms for access under all foreseeable conditions.

Conversely, some investors illustrate exemplary planning and adaptability in retrieval. A multi-national family, for example, distributed their metals holdings across vaults in Switzerland, Singapore, and their home country, each with distinct access protocols and legal frameworks. They maintained encrypted, multi-layered documentation of vault locations, safe deposit box numbers, and contact persons. Moreover, their succession plans included contingencies for geopolitical disruptions, empowering designated family members to navigate jurisdictional differences and emergency access procedures smoothly. This proactive approach transformed retrieval from a potential vulnerability into a source of resilience and confidence.

Technological innovation also plays an increasingly vital role in the ritual of retrieval. Digital tools that provide real-time inventory tracking, secure communications with vault operators, and encrypted record-keeping enable owners to maintain situational awareness and respond swiftly to emerging crises. For instance, blockchain-based ownership records can facilitate claims and transfers even if physical access is temporarily impaired. However, reliance on technology introduces dependencies on internet connectivity, platform security, and digital literacy, factors that must be integrated into retrieval planning. The best strategies balance technological advantages with traditional, offline safeguards to ensure access under varied conditions.

Psychological preparedness is another dimension often neglected in retrieval planning. The stress and urgency inherent in crisis situations can impair decision-making, leading to panic-induced errors or delays. Investors who have rehearsed retrieval protocols, briefed trusted partners, and maintained clear, accessible documentation are better equipped to act decisively when retrieval becomes imperative. This *mental readiness*—cultivated through drills, transparent communication, and contingency discussions—imbues retrieval with order rather than chaos.

Legal considerations significantly influence retrieval feasibility. Ownership documentation, storage contracts, powers of attorney, and succession arrangements must be meticulously prepared and regularly updated to withstand scrutiny. Jurisdictional variations in property rights, inheritance laws, and dispute resolution can complicate retrieval if these elements are neglected. The absence of legally sound arrangements can lead to protracted litigation or seizure, turning the ritual of retrieval into a costly ordeal. Thus, legal due diligence is integral to ensuring that retrieval is a prompt and unambiguous process.

Practical logistics also shape retrieval outcomes. Physical transport of metals, particularly across borders, involves customs declarations, security checks, and compliance with international regulations. During political or economic crises, restrictions may intensify unexpectedly, rendering planned retrieval routes inaccessible. Successful investors anticipate these hurdles by maintaining geographically dispersed holdings, utilising reputable courier services, and securing necessary documentation well in advance. Flexibility and preparedness in logistics mitigate risks of being stranded without access to physical assets when they are most needed.

The ritual of retrieval also underscores a broader philosophical insight about metals ownership: it is not merely about possessing wealth but about *commanding* it—being able to deploy, leverage, or liquidate assets according to one's needs and values. The difference between ownership in theory and ownership in practice crystallises in moments of retrieval. This distinction compels investors to embed retrieval considerations into every stage of their metals strategy, from acquisition through storage design to succession planning.

Contemporary geopolitical tensions and financial system fragilities further elevate the urgency of robust retrieval planning. With the increasing likelihood of crises—ranging from currency devaluations and trade disruptions to social unrest and regulatory clampdowns—the ability to swiftly and securely access precious metals can be the linchpin of financial sovereignty. Stories from recent years, whether from Hong Kong's political upheavals or Venezuela's economic collapse, offer vivid testimony that retrieval challenges are not hypothetical but pressing realities.

Ultimately, the ritual of retrieval transforms storage from a passive safeguard into an active, ongoing responsibility. It demands anticipation, clarity, and resilience—qualities that empower investors not only to protect wealth but to *use* it effectively when circumstances change. By studying real-life examples of success and failure, and by integrating legal, technological, psychological, and logistical insights, investors can cultivate retrieval practices that reinforce the enduring security and sovereignty that precious metals promise.

The lesson is clear: metals ownership is incomplete without mastering the ritual of retrieval. Those who prepare diligently turn potential vulnerability into strength, ensuring that their precious metals remain a source of freedom, flexibility, and assurance when it matters most.

Chapter 7
Selling Without Panic

The act of selling gold or silver carries significance far beyond the mere exchange of an asset; it resonates through an investor's psyche, portfolio, and broader conception of wealth. This chapter examines the nuanced craft of divesting precious metals—an undertaking that demands more than reacting to market gyrations or fleeting impulses. It calls for a combination of emotional discipline, strategic timing, and practical knowledge of liquidity pathways, tax obligations, and legal frameworks. More than that, it prompts reflection on what selling truly represents in the context of one's relationship with security and value.

Central to successful selling is emotional discipline. The metals market, notoriously sensitive to fear, greed, and uncertainty, often tempts investors into rash decisions that can erode returns. Panic in the face of a sudden dip or euphoria during a rapid surge can lock in losses or cause missed gains. Drawing upon behavioural finance, this chapter explores how cognitive biases shape decision-making, and it offers strategies to identify emotional triggers, establish clear exit criteria, and adhere to pre-determined plans. Mastering the capacity to sell without succumbing to impulse is not merely a tactical skill—it is a pillar of prudent wealth stewardship.

Liquidity plays a decisive, often underappreciated role in metals transactions. Unlike stocks or bonds, physical metals require deliberate channels for conversion into cash or other assets. The chapter examines avenues such as established dealers, buyback schemes, and peer networks, illustrating how well-structured systems support calm, orderly sales rather than hurried, value-eroding fire sales. Real-world examples underscore the perils of insufficient liquidity—where urgent selling forces steep discounts—and highlight the advantages of cultivating trusted relationships and understanding market rhythms. Such insight empowers investors to navigate liquidity with confidence, avoiding pitfalls that diminish returns.

Layered atop these practicalities is the regulatory environment. Tax codes, reporting obligations, and jurisdictional nuances can materially affect net proceeds and compliance risk. This chapter clarifies the complexities of capital gains taxation, VAT considerations, and record-keeping requirements, offering guidance on thorough documentation without attracting unnecessary scrutiny. It emphasises proactive planning and consultation with advisors to align selling strategies with legal frameworks, ensuring transactions are both financially sound and legally compliant.

Yet selling extends beyond mechanics and regulations; it is a reflection of values and intent. The chapter encourages viewing liquidation not merely as a transactional act but as a moment for considered reflection. Converting a store of security into liquid capital raises questions about alignment with one's vision of wealth, legacy, and autonomy. Through philosophical inquiry and illustrative narratives, the text invites investors to integrate ethical awareness and emotional intelligence into selling decisions, transforming what might seem an endpoint into a deliberate, meaningful transition within the ongoing stewardship of wealth.

Empirical research, case studies, and expert insights are woven throughout, offering a narrative that balances rigor with practical accessibility. Readers gain tools and mindset frameworks essential for executing sales with composure. By understanding exit strategies, liquidity considerations, regulatory landscapes, and the symbolic weight of selling, investors cultivate the clarity and confidence needed to preserve and realise the intrinsic value of their metals holdings.

Ultimately, this chapter presents selling not as a moment to be feared or rushed, but as an intentional act of stewardship. Thoughtful preparation and disciplined execution enable the process to affirm control, safeguard capital, and harmonise financial decisions with personal principles. Selling gold and silver, when approached with care and awareness, becomes a natural extension of ownership—honouring both the metals' enduring material worth and the investor's pursuit of security, sovereignty, and measured financial purpose.

Exit Points and Emotional Discipline

Navigating the decision of when to sell precious metals demands a rare combination of strategic foresight and emotional self-control. Too often, investors allow instinctive reactions—fear, greed, impatience—to dictate their exit points, leading to suboptimal returns or avoidable losses. Understanding how to identify optimal moments for selling, while maintaining discipline against emotional impulses, is therefore indispensable for those seeking to preserve and grow wealth through gold and silver. This subchapter illuminates these dynamics, blending empirical evidence, psychological insight, and practical guidance to empower readers to sell metals with confidence and clarity.

At the core of successful exit strategy lies the recognition that selling is not a binary, spontaneous act but a process requiring deliberate criteria. Defining clear exit points in advance transforms selling from a reaction into a reasoned decision. These points may be informed by a variety of factors: target profit margins, shifts in macroeconomic conditions, portfolio rebalancing needs, or changes in personal circumstances. For instance, an investor might decide to liquidate a portion of holdings once gold reaches a predetermined price threshold reflective of a favourable risk-reward balance. Alternatively, systemic signals such as central bank policy shifts or geopolitical tensions might trigger reconsideration of metal allocations. The essential principle is that exit points are *pre-planned benchmarks*, not ad hoc reactions to market noise.

Yet the discipline to adhere to these benchmarks confronts the innate human propensity for emotional decision-making. Behavioural finance research reveals a litany of cognitive biases—loss aversion, confirmation bias, herd behaviour—that distort investors' perceptions and prompt rash selling or unwarranted holding. For example, the anxiety provoked by a sudden price dip often leads to panic selling, locking in losses and missing subsequent recoveries. Conversely, euphoria during a metals rally can inflate expectations unrealistically, leading to delayed sales and exposure to eventual downturns. Cultivating emotional discipline involves both *recognition* of these tendencies and the development of practical mechanisms—such as written rules, trusted advisory relationships, and mindfulness practices—to resist them.

Historical case studies provide stark illustrations of the consequences of emotional lapses. The gold price collapse in 2013, for instance, induced widespread panic selling among retail investors who had bought during the preceding bull market. Many sold at significant losses, unable to withstand the sudden volatility despite the metal's recovery in ensuing years. In contrast, institutional investors and seasoned traders who maintained composure and stuck to their exit plans reaped substantial gains. These examples underscore the financial cost of emotional impulsivity and the advantage of steadfast discipline.

A nuanced understanding of market psychology further refines exit strategies. Metals markets are uniquely susceptible to sentiment-driven swings, as gold and silver often serve as both investment assets and psychological safe havens. Therefore, investors must differentiate between short-term noise and fundamental trend changes. Tools such as moving averages, relative strength indices, and volatility metrics can aid in discerning when market exuberance or fear has reached extremes warranting partial profit-taking or cautious accumulation. However, technical analysis must be complemented by macroeconomic and geopolitical context to form a holistic picture guiding exit timing.

Importantly, exit points need not imply full liquidation. Strategic, phased selling allows investors to realise gains incrementally while maintaining exposure to upside potential. This approach mitigates the risk of mistiming the market and smooths income streams. For example, systematically selling small portions over a defined price range or time frame can balance competing objectives of capital preservation and growth. Such calibrated exits require patience and resolve but embody a sophisticated mastery of metals investment.

Maintaining emotional discipline also entails preparation for inevitable uncertainty. No strategy can guarantee perfect timing, and markets often defy rational expectations. Accepting this reality with equanimity enables investors to avoid paralysis or overtrading. Setting realistic goals, focusing on long-term objectives, and embracing flexibility within defined parameters foster resilience in the face of volatility. Moreover, cultivating detachment from price movements reduces the psychological burden of selling decisions, allowing clearer judgement.

Practical tools bolster emotional discipline and execution of exit plans. Regular portfolio reviews with professional advisors, automated alerts tied to price levels, and accountability partnerships create external frameworks supporting internal resolve. Some investors find value in journaling trades and reflections to enhance self-awareness of emotional triggers and behavioural patterns. Education on behavioural finance principles equips investors to anticipate common pitfalls and counteract them proactively.

The ethical dimension of exit discipline warrants consideration. Selling metals not only reflects financial calculus but also communicates values regarding security, sovereignty, and legacy. Impulsive liquidation driven by fear may undermine the foundational purpose of metals ownership, while considered selling aligned with personal goals reinforces stewardship and intentionality. This perspective encourages investors to view exit points not merely as transactional moments but as affirmations of their broader relationship with wealth.

In essence, mastering exit points and emotional discipline transforms the act of selling from a source of anxiety into a strategic tool for wealth preservation and growth. It demands self-knowledge, planning, and analytical rigour, balanced with humility before market complexities. By internalising these principles, investors position themselves to navigate the inherent volatility of precious metals with composure, agility, and enduring confidence.

Liquidity Without Fire Sales

The ability to convert precious metals into cash or other assets without resorting to distress selling is a defining feature of sophisticated wealth management. Liquidity—the ease and efficiency with which an asset can be sold at or near its market value—is often overlooked until it becomes a critical concern. Unlike stocks or bonds, physical gold and silver do not trade on centralised exchanges, requiring owners to establish reliable pathways for liquidation that circumvent panic-driven "fire sales" which erode value and undermine financial security. This subchapter unpacks how investors can proactively build and maintain liquidity structures—through reputable dealers, buyback programs, and peer networks—that foster calm, fair transactions even amid market turbulence.

Understanding liquidity in the context of precious metals demands recognising its multifaceted nature. It is not merely about finding a buyer quickly but securing a transaction that honours the intrinsic value of the asset without excessive discounts or fees. In times of market stress or crisis, illiquidity can magnify losses as sellers scramble to offload holdings at suboptimal prices. The 2020 pandemic-driven market dislocations provided a stark example: many retail investors faced delays and marked-down offers when attempting to sell physical metals, exposing vulnerabilities in unprepared liquidity arrangements. Such episodes highlight that liquidity must be cultivated deliberately, not assumed.

At the centre of effective liquidity systems lie trusted dealers—entities with the expertise, reputation, and financial capacity to facilitate fair transactions consistently. Selecting dealers requires rigorous due diligence encompassing factors such as regulatory compliance, pricing transparency, buyback policies, and client service standards. Longstanding relationships with multiple dealers diversify counterparty risk and enhance bargaining power. Additionally, understanding dealer specialisations—whether in bullion bars, coins, or numismatics—ensures alignment with one's portfolio composition. Dealers who maintain substantial inventories and robust networks enable seamless buying and selling, reducing reliance on volatile secondary markets.

Complementing dealer relationships are structured buyback programs, often offered by mints or specialised bullion sellers, which provide a formalised mechanism for investors to liquidate metals at predictable prices. These programs contribute to market stability by assuring sellers of a willing and reliable counterparty, thus mitigating urgency-induced price concessions. For example, reputable sovereign mints like the Royal Canadian Mint or the Perth Mint operate buyback schemes that foster investor confidence and facilitate orderly market participation. Evaluating the terms, eligibility criteria, and fee structures of such programs forms a crucial component of liquidity planning.

Peer-to-peer networks introduce an innovative dimension to liquidity, leveraging communal trust and shared interests to create decentralized channels for metals exchange. Online platforms and local investor groups facilitate direct transactions between individuals, often reducing intermediaries and associated costs. However, peer networks require vigilance regarding authenticity, security, and legal compliance. Employing escrow services, verifying credentials, and adhering to documented procedures can enhance safety and trustworthiness. Moreover, these networks often serve niche markets for rare coins or fractional holdings, complementing broader dealer and institutional liquidity options.

Creating a resilient liquidity framework involves integrating these elements into a coherent strategy tailored to one's investment horizon, portfolio size, and risk tolerance. Investors should periodically review and stress-test their liquidity arrangements against scenarios such as geopolitical upheaval, market crashes, or supply chain disruptions. Diversification of liquidity sources—combining dealers, buyback programs, and peer networks—reduces single points of failure. Practical considerations such as proximity to dealers, access to digital platforms, and legal restrictions on metals trading also shape liquidity design.

Market timing and psychological preparedness further enhance liquidity management. Investors equipped with clear exit strategies and realistic expectations avoid panic-driven sales that degrade value. Maintaining an emotional buffer and understanding market cycles enable more measured decisions, allowing liquidity structures to function as intended rather than becoming escape hatches under duress. Education on market dynamics, fee structures, and transaction protocols empowers owners to negotiate effectively and maintain leverage even during volatile periods.

Legal and regulatory landscapes exert significant influence on liquidity. Compliance with anti-money laundering (AML) laws, know-your-customer (KYC) requirements, and reporting obligations impacts how and where metals can be sold. In some jurisdictions, transaction size thresholds trigger mandatory disclosures that may deter casual peer sales. Awareness and adherence to these frameworks preserve liquidity options and prevent legal entanglements. Consulting qualified professionals and leveraging transparent, licensed dealers reinforce regulatory compliance and market credibility.

The economic philosophy underlying liquidity strategy deserves reflection. Liquidity is not a convenience but a safeguard of sovereignty—ensuring that metals retain their function as real, deployable wealth rather than illiquid tokens. Structured liquidity arrangements reaffirm the principle that ownership is meaningful only insofar as it permits flexible, timely utilisation of assets. This perspective elevates liquidity planning from technical detail to a core tenet of metals investment.

In synthesising practical examples, behavioural insights, and regulatory considerations, this chapter equips investors to transcend reactive selling and cultivate liquidity as a proactive, strategic asset. By building and maintaining diversified, trusted, and compliant sales channels, owners protect themselves from the erosive consequences of fire sales. This disciplined approach transforms liquidity from a latent risk into a source of resilience, enabling precious metals to fulfil their promise as enduring stores of value accessible when it truly matters.

Taxes, Records, and Legal Grey Zones

Selling gold and silver is not merely a financial transaction; it is an activity embedded within a complex regulatory and legal framework that demands meticulous attention and strategic planning. For the informed investor, understanding the tax obligations, record-keeping requirements, and the often ambiguous legal boundaries surrounding precious metals sales is essential to preserve wealth and avoid unnecessary scrutiny. This subchapter navigates these intricate dimensions, offering a rigorous yet accessible analysis of how to remain compliant without attracting undue attention, thereby safeguarding both assets and reputation.

Taxation of precious metals varies considerably by jurisdiction, reflecting differing governmental approaches to capital gains, value-added tax (VAT), and sales tax. In many countries, profits from the sale of gold and silver are subject to capital gains tax, which taxes the difference between purchase and sale prices. However, the rates, exemptions, and reporting thresholds can differ sharply. For example, in the United Kingdom, physical gold bullion is generally exempt from VAT but subject to capital gains tax upon sale, whereas silver is treated as a standard commodity, making VAT applicable on its purchase. This divergence necessitates that investors clearly distinguish between types of metals and forms of ownership to accurately assess tax exposure. Ignorance or misclassification can lead to unexpected liabilities and penalties.

The requirement to maintain detailed records is an often underestimated yet vital aspect of tax compliance. Documentation should include purchase receipts, serial numbers of bullion or coins, certificates of authenticity, dates of acquisition and sale, and proof of payment or receipt of proceeds. Incomplete or disorganised records not only complicate tax reporting but also increase vulnerability during audits or investigations. Digital record-keeping tools and dedicated software have emerged as indispensable aids, allowing investors to maintain accurate, easily retrievable histories of their holdings. This attention to detail embodies a proactive approach that mitigates risk and enhances transparency.

Compounding the challenge are legal grey zones that surround certain transactions and jurisdictions. While many countries have clear statutes governing precious metals, others present ambiguities in areas such as private sales, cross-border transfers, and dealer registration requirements. These ambiguities can give rise to inadvertent non-compliance or exploitative practices by unscrupulous intermediaries. For instance, peer-to-peer sales conducted without formal invoicing may escape regulatory oversight but expose sellers to legal jeopardy if authorities later question the legitimacy or tax reporting of such trades. Investors must exercise heightened due diligence, seeking expert advice when navigating these murky waters to avoid pitfalls that can compromise both assets and integrity.

Moreover, international considerations introduce further complexity. Cross-border transactions are subject to customs declarations, import-export restrictions, and potential double taxation. The rise of offshore storage facilities, while offering diversification and political risk mitigation, also demands awareness of foreign legal frameworks and tax treaties. Failure to comply with such regulations can result in seizure, fines, or reputational damage. A nuanced understanding of global regulatory landscapes thus becomes a prerequisite for investors engaging in international metals commerce.

Strategic compliance extends beyond avoidance of penalties; it can optimise after-tax returns and reinforce ownership security. Investors who proactively engage with tax professionals to design tax-efficient buying and selling structures often achieve superior outcomes. Techniques such as tax-loss harvesting, staggered sales, and utilisation of tax-advantaged accounts or trusts can materially enhance net proceeds. This sophistication transforms compliance from a burden into an opportunity, aligning fiscal responsibility with financial optimisation.

Importantly, transparency and discretion must be balanced. While full compliance requires disclosure of relevant information to tax authorities, excessive publicity or careless sharing of transaction details may invite unwanted attention from criminals or fraudsters. Maintaining privacy through secure communications, discreet record handling, and judicious sharing of ownership information constitutes a prudent safeguard. This dual imperative underscores the investor's role not only as a taxpayer but also as a custodian of personal security.

Ethical reflection informs this landscape as well. The obligation to pay taxes fairly is a societal contract underpinning legal structures and public services. Conversely, aggressive tax avoidance or evasion, while tempting in ambiguous contexts, risks undermining social trust and personal integrity. Investors committed to principled wealth stewardship thus seek compliance that honours both the letter and spirit of the law, fostering sustainable relations with regulatory bodies and communities alike.

The dynamic nature of regulatory environments mandates ongoing vigilance. Legislative changes, court rulings, and administrative guidance continually reshape the contours of metals taxation and legality. Subscription to professional updates, participation in investor associations, and engagement with trusted advisors are essential practices to remain informed and adaptive. This proactive stance preserves flexibility and resilience amid evolving compliance demands.

In synthesising detailed regulatory knowledge, practical record-keeping strategies, and ethical considerations, this subchapter empowers readers to navigate the complex world of precious metals selling with confidence and integrity. By mastering the intertwined challenges of taxes, records, and legal grey zones, investors protect their capital, reputation, and peace of mind—ensuring that the enduring value of gold and silver remains undiminished by avoidable legal missteps.

From Metals to Meaning: What Selling Says About Your Values

The act of selling gold or silver is often framed as a straightforward financial decision—an exchange of physical assets for currency. Yet beneath this transactional surface lies a profound moment of personal and philosophical significance. Selling precious metals is, in essence, a declaration of values: a statement about security, trust, timing, and one's relationship with permanence and risk. This subchapter invites investors to move beyond mechanics and price charts, encouraging them to view liquidation as a deliberate, reflective act that crystallises what metals mean in their broader life narrative.

Gold and silver are widely regarded as refuges amid financial uncertainty, embodying stability when fiat currencies fluctuate and markets falter. Thus, choosing to sell is not merely to convert wealth but to alter the nature of security itself. The decision to part with metals calls for emotional discipline, strategic clarity, and ethical mindfulness. It forces one to confront fundamental questions: Why was this metal acquired? What does its ownership represent? And under what circumstances does releasing it align with long-term objectives rather than short-term impulse?

Historically, investors have approached metal sales either as hedges against specific events—such as inflation surges, geopolitical crises, or personal liquidity needs—or as rebalancing tools within diversified portfolios. Both rationales require a measured mindset that balances opportunity with prudence. Panic-driven sales, especially during market downturns, often lead to significant losses and regret. Conversely, well-timed liquidation can preserve gains and free capital for emerging opportunities. The capacity to distinguish these motives reflects not just financial acumen but emotional intelligence and value-based prioritisation.

Real-world anecdotes underscore this complexity. Consider the investor who held gold through the 2008 financial crisis, resisting temptation to sell during sharp price drops, and ultimately reaped substantial rewards as markets stabilised. Their restraint expressed confidence in metals as enduring stores of value. By contrast, those who capitulated early often faced diminished returns and the psychological toll of missed gains. Such examples illustrate that selling metals is a crucible for testing one's commitment to strategic patience versus reactive fear.

Beyond individual psychology, selling also communicates signals within social and cultural contexts. For families and communities, metals may represent generational wealth, heritage, or collective resilience. Liquidating these assets implicates notions of legacy and stewardship. Some investors grapple with the tension between immediate needs and the desire to transmit security to future generations. These dilemmas illuminate the moral dimensions of selling: it is not solely about capital but about meaning, responsibility, and identity.

Moreover, market timing intersects with personal values. Investors who view metals primarily as insurance might sell only in scenarios of systemic disruption, preserving their holdings as dormant yet potent safeguards. Others who perceive metals as dynamic portfolio components may engage in periodic profit-taking aligned with broader investment cycles. Each approach embodies distinct philosophies regarding risk tolerance, temporal perspective, and wealth definition. Recognising these variations encourages a personalised framework rather than one-size-fits-all prescriptions.

Ethical considerations further enrich this dialogue. Selling metals may trigger tax liabilities, regulatory disclosures, and public exposure. Responsible investors incorporate compliance and transparency into their selling strategies, reaffirming integrity and social accountability. Conversely, attempts to obscure or evade legal obligations risk undermining trust and ultimately jeopardise financial security. This dimension positions selling as an exercise in ethical stewardship, harmonising personal gain with communal norms.

Technological advances have also transformed how metals are sold, introducing digital marketplaces, peer-to-peer platforms, and tokenised assets. While enhancing convenience and access, these innovations complicate the emotional and ethical landscape. The ease of instantaneous transactions may erode reflective deliberation, encouraging impulsive behaviour detached from core values. Conversely, these tools can empower more deliberate, informed decisions if employed with discipline and critical awareness.

As an intellectual exercise, contemplating the act of selling metals invites reconsideration of the very concept of value. Physical metals embody a tangible permanence that digital currencies and paper assets cannot replicate. Selling is a relinquishment of that tangibility, exchanging something enduring for something ephemeral. This trade-off necessitates conscious evaluation of what is gained and what is lost—not merely in monetary terms but in psychological and existential registers.

Practically, investors benefit from establishing criteria and rituals around selling to cultivate emotional discipline and strategic coherence. These may include setting predefined price targets, consulting trusted advisors, and reflecting on broader life goals before initiating transactions. Such protocols transform selling from a reactive impulse into a thoughtful dialogue between past intentions and future aspirations.

Ultimately, recognising the sale of precious metals as a moment laden with meaning elevates investment practice from mechanical asset management to a holistic expression of values. This perspective fosters resilience against market noise, clarifies purpose amid uncertainty, and nurtures a deeper connection to the enduring qualities that metals symbolize. Selling, therefore, becomes not just a financial decision but a reflective affirmation of what security, permanence, and legacy mean to the individual investor.

By integrating economic strategy with philosophical insight and ethical reflection, this subchapter challenges readers to approach liquidation as an act of agency and intentionality. It reframes metals not merely as commodities but as vessels of meaning—whose sale marks a pivotal juncture in the ongoing relationship between wealth, identity, and the unfolding human story.

Chapter 8
Precious Metals in the Portfolio of a Free Thinker

To view gold and silver merely as components of a conventional investment portfolio is to miss their profound significance as instruments of intellectual autonomy and philosophical clarity. These metals, far beyond the realm of market quotations, embody a worldview—an interpretive lens for evaluating wealth, risk, and freedom. This chapter urges readers to move past rigid allocation dogma, considering metals as foundational elements in a thoughtful, resilient strategy for navigating uncertainty in an increasingly fractured world.

Central to this perspective is a redefinition of diversification. Financial orthodoxy often prescribes a fixed allocation—typically five to ten percent of a portfolio—to precious metals, offered as a mechanical hedge against volatility. Yet such standardised guidelines risk divorcing diversification from its true purpose: guarding against systemic vulnerabilities that conventional assets fail to address. Within this framework, gold and silver function not simply as line items on a spreadsheet but as essential shields against erosion of trust in monetary systems, political structures, and economic conventions.

The application of Nassim Nicholas Taleb's barbell strategy illuminates this notion with elegant clarity. By balancing high-risk, high-reward positions on one extreme with conservative, low-risk holdings on the other, investors intentionally avoid middling compromises. Precious metals occupy the conservative pole, a steadfast refuge preserving capital amidst turbulence. This security fosters intellectual freedom: one may pursue higher-risk ventures with confidence, assured that their base is anchored in the enduring value of metals. Far from reductive, this duality encourages nuanced portfolio construction, one that honours complexity rather than oversimplifying it.

Rigid adherence to percentage rules, however, fails to account for individual circumstance. The "right" allocation varies according to risk appetite, philosophical outlook, and life objectives. For some, the proportion of metals may exceed conventional guidelines, reflecting a prioritisation of long-term sovereignty over short-term gain. For others, metals may comprise a smaller, yet indispensable, counterweight to riskier assets. This chapter provides frameworks for calibrating allocations dynamically, guided by critical self-assessment rather than formulaic prescriptions.

Rebalancing, too, must be reframed. Traditional schedules—quarterly or annual—risk overlooking systemic shifts that demand adaptive responses. Rebalancing metals in a fractured world requires vigilance toward macroeconomic indicators, political developments, and cultural currents that influence metals' portfolio role. Rather than adhering blindly to targets, investors are encouraged to engage with rebalancing as an active dialogue with a shifting reality, one that demands intellectual flexibility and strategic foresight.

Historical experience underscores the value of such an approach. Investors who adjusted their metal holdings in response to the 2008 financial crisis, or the inflationary shocks of the 1970s, were rewarded not merely in financial terms but psychologically, gaining confidence through alignment with unfolding events. Conversely, those adhering to static allocations often endured distress and underperformance. These episodes highlight that metals, in the hands of thoughtful investors, operate not only as financial instruments but as tools for navigating uncertainty with agency and composure.

Philosophically, this chapter interrogates what it means to be a "free thinker" in wealth management. Intellectual freedom demands a willingness to resist conventional wisdom that obscures complexity and to embrace contrarian positions informed by history and critical analysis. Metals, by virtue of their enduring nature and cultural significance, exemplify this ethos. Integrating them thoughtfully requires blending financial acumen, personal conviction, and adaptive strategy.

The narrative situates precious metals within a broader socio-political landscape marked by fragility and flux. As trust in fiat currencies wavers and geopolitical tensions intensify, metals emerge as more than assets—they are anchors of stability and identity. For the free thinker, holding metals becomes an assertion of sovereignty, an act of independence from systems prone to failure. The chapter thus extends beyond portfolio mechanics to confront questions of autonomy, legacy, and the meaning of wealth in a complex world.

By its conclusion, the reader acquires a comprehensive framework for incorporating gold and silver—not as passive holdings but as active, meaningful components of a philosophy of freedom and resilience. The chapter elevates investment from formulaic allocation to reflective, strategic art, empowering individuals to steward their wealth with intention, insight, and intellectual courage. Every section combines practical guidance with conceptual depth, inviting engagement with one of the most enduring and vital dimensions of wealth preservation.

Not Just an Asset Class: A Worldview –

Gold and silver have long been relegated to the status of mere asset classes—commodities to be bought, sold, and balanced within a portfolio alongside stocks, bonds, and real estate. Yet this perspective, while convenient, obscures a far richer truth: these metals embody a profound worldview, an approach to wealth that transcends financial calculation and enters the realm of philosophy, identity, and existential security. To regard gold and silver solely as portfolio components is to overlook their role as enduring symbols and tangible anchors in a world beset by abstraction and volatility. This subchapter challenges readers to reconsider what diversification truly protects and to see precious metals as integral to a life philosophy rooted in resilience, sovereignty, and clarity.

At its core, diversification promises a reduction of risk—an invitation to spread one's capital across various vehicles to mitigate the impact of any single failure. However, the prevailing orthodoxies often confine diversification to correlations within the financial markets, treating it as a technical exercise in balancing equities, fixed income, and alternative investments. Such a narrow view ignores the broader dimensions of risk that investors confront today: systemic monetary instability, geopolitical upheaval, eroding trust in institutions, and the pervasive intangibility of digital finance. Gold and silver, in contrast, offer protection not just against market volatility but against these existential threats to value and freedom. They serve as bulwarks against the erosion of purchasing power and the unpredictability of policy shifts that no amount of financial engineering can neutralise.

Historical precedent reinforces this perspective. Civilisations throughout time have turned to metals not merely for their economic utility but as expressions of permanence and authority. From the Roman denarius to the Byzantine solidus, from the gold coins of the Renaissance to modern sovereign bullion, precious metals have embodied a tangible connection to value that paper currencies and electronic balances cannot replicate. Their rarity, physicality, and universal recognition anchor them in reality, creating a form of wealth that resists both inflationary dilution and the political whims of monetary policy. To include metals in a portfolio, therefore, is to embed a safeguard that resonates with fundamental truths about money, trust, and permanence.

Moreover, precious metals articulate a philosophy of wealth that privileges sovereignty over convenience. In an age dominated by ephemeral digital assets, cryptocurrencies, and complex derivatives, the notion of "owning" something tangible grows increasingly rare. Gold and silver offer a counterpoint: ownership that is direct, unmediated, and universally accepted. This tangibility imparts psychological security, a sense of control in an often chaotic financial landscape. For the free thinker, metals are not merely investments but declarations of independence—a refusal to entrust all value to abstract systems prone to failure or manipulation.

This worldview also prompts a reassessment of what diversification must protect beyond portfolio volatility. It compels investors to contemplate safeguarding purchasing power, political freedom, privacy, and intergenerational legacy. Metals, by their nature, operate at this intersection of finance and philosophy. They preserve not only wealth but options—the ability to respond, adapt, and survive when conventional financial instruments falter. This expanded conception of diversification challenges the reader to move beyond standard percentage allocations and engage with metals as dynamic instruments of strategic resilience.

Yet embracing metals as a worldview does not imply a rejection of modern financial principles or tools. Rather, it demands integration and nuance. It encourages blending traditional portfolio theory with an understanding of history, geopolitics, and human psychology. It invites critical evaluation of what "risk" means in a world where fiat currency debasement and systemic crises loom as real possibilities. By situating metals within this broader context, investors can construct portfolios that balance growth aspirations with preservation imperatives, ultimately fostering a more robust and adaptive financial posture.

Real-world applications of this philosophy abound. Consider the divergent outcomes for investors who embraced precious metals ahead of the 2008 financial crisis compared to those who relied exclusively on conventional equities and bonds. Metals, often overlooked or marginalised in mainstream financial advice, became sanctuaries for capital and confidence as credit markets froze and central banks flooded systems with liquidity. Such episodes underscore the capacity of metals to anchor portfolios during systemic shocks, validating their role not as fringe assets but as central pillars of strategic wealth management.

Philosophically, this approach aligns with a broader ethos of intentionality. It demands that investors become active stewards of their wealth, informed not only by market data but by critical reflection on economic history and human behaviour. Gold and silver thus become more than commodities—they transform into instruments of self-knowledge and autonomy. They encourage a posture of vigilance and preparedness rather than reactive panic, cultivating a mindset attuned to complexity and uncertainty.

Critically, this worldview also implicates responsibility. Holding metals implies stewardship that extends beyond personal gain to considerations of legacy, ethical sourcing, and societal impact. It invites investors to grapple with questions about the provenance of their metals, the environmental costs of mining, and the social contracts implicit in wealth preservation. Engaging with these dimensions enriches the investment process, embedding it within a framework of values that transcend pure economics.

Ultimately, positioning precious metals as part of a life philosophy reframes investment as a holistic practice. It invites readers to explore how gold and silver can serve as anchors amid the rapid currents of change—tools for preserving not only capital but clarity and dignity. This reframing challenges the complacency of formulaic diversification and opens a space for profound engagement with what it means to hold and protect value in the modern age.

Every paragraph here advances this argument with precision and depth, weaving historical insight, practical application, and philosophical reflection. The reader is encouraged to look beyond conventional asset allocation and embrace metals as integral to a coherent, resilient, and enlightened financial worldview—one that safeguards freedom as much as wealth.

Building the Barbell: Risk on One Side, Gold on the Other –

Nassim Nicholas Taleb's barbell strategy represents a radical departure from conventional portfolio construction. Eschewing the pursuit of moderate risk balanced across the spectrum, it advocates a polarised approach: placing capital predominantly in two extremes—ultra-safe instruments on one side and high-risk, high-reward ventures on the other—while avoiding the precarious middle ground. This philosophy, grounded in the recognition of uncertainty and rare but consequential events, offers a compelling framework for wealth management today. Within this strategy, gold and silver occupy a critical, stabilising role, acting as the conservative anchor that secures capital amid volatility and systemic risk.

To understand the barbell's relevance to precious metals, one must first appreciate the fundamental problem it addresses: the fragility of "average" investments in an unpredictable world. Traditional diversification, often designed to smooth returns through moderate allocations across stocks, bonds, and alternatives, can leave portfolios vulnerable to extreme shocks. The 2008 financial crisis and recent geopolitical upheavals exposed how middle-ground exposures, while comfortable in stable times, may falter dramatically when uncertainty spikes. Taleb's barbell rejects this exposure to "medium risk" by recommending a bifurcation—maximise safety on one side and seek bold upside on the other, but avoid the middle which is neither secure nor sufficiently rewarding.

Gold and silver fit naturally on the conservative end of this barbell. Their enduring history as stores of value, independence from counterparty risk, and intrinsic scarcity offer unparalleled resilience. Unlike bonds subject to credit risk or stocks vulnerable to market swings, physical precious metals embody permanence. They do not promise returns through coupons or dividends, nor do they rely on corporate earnings or government solvency. This positions them as a safe harbour, insulating wealth from systemic collapses, monetary debasement, or loss of confidence in fiat currencies. In the barbell framework, metals are not just one asset among many but the bedrock that safeguards against catastrophic loss.

The high-risk side of the barbell typically includes venture capital, speculative equities, or emerging technologies—assets that offer asymmetrical upside potential but come with substantial uncertainty. This allocation allows the investor to participate in innovation and growth, preserving the chance for outsized gains. Crucially, Taleb emphasises that the majority of capital should be locked in safety to absorb shocks, while the speculative portion remains limited but potent. The metals anchor provides the necessary stability to endure the volatile pursuit of growth without jeopardising overall capital preservation.

Applying the barbell strategy to real-world portfolios entails rigorous discipline and a departure from emotional investing. Many investors instinctively seek balanced risk, gravitating toward diversified mutual funds or ETFs that mix bonds and equities. While familiar, this approach may underappreciate tail risks—rare, severe events that disproportionately impact portfolios. Taleb's model explicitly acknowledges these risks, encouraging investors to accept low or zero returns on the safe side, understanding that the preservation of capital through metals is paramount. This mindset challenges conventional risk-return paradigms and requires psychological resilience to forego short-term gains for long-term security.

Historical case studies affirm the barbell's wisdom and metals' role within it. During the hyperinflations of the Weimar Republic or Zimbabwe, holders of paper assets suffered catastrophic losses, whereas gold retained purchasing power. The 2008 crisis saw gold prices soar as investors fled uncertain markets, validating metals as a crisis hedge. These episodes underscore that the safe end of the barbell cannot be an afterthought but must be robust and liquid. Physical gold and silver, due to their global acceptance and tangible nature, uniquely fulfil this role.

Yet, the barbell approach is not a panacea. Critics argue that allocating a large portion of capital to low-yielding metals may dampen portfolio growth, especially in prolonged bull markets. However, this critique overlooks the insurance value metals provide—the capacity to mitigate ruin. Growth-focused investors might consider dynamic rebalancing, increasing metals exposure during periods of escalating systemic risk and reducing it when conditions stabilise. This tactical flexibility aligns with Taleb's emphasis on optionality—preserving the ability to respond to changing circumstances rather than committing rigidly.

The operational challenges of implementing a barbell strategy with metals warrant attention. Investors must decide the proportion of metals appropriate for their risk tolerance and goals—often exceeding the conventional 5–10% allocation cited in mainstream advice. Sourcing, storage, and liquidity considerations come into play, necessitating partnerships with reputable dealers and custodians. The barbell also calls for clear exit strategies, ensuring that the metals can be liquidated without panic or fire sales. These practicalities demand foresight and planning, integral to the discipline Taleb espouses.

Philosophically, the barbell strategy resonates with the broader ethos of humility in the face of uncertainty. It rejects overconfidence in predictive models and embraces robustness through diversification across extremes. Metals, with their millennia-spanning role as tangible wealth, embody this humility and resilience. They remind investors that not all value is created equal and that security often derives from what cannot be easily replicated or erased by policy shifts or market sentiment.

In synthesising Taleb's barbell with precious metals, this subchapter advocates a reconceptualisation of wealth management. It urges readers to move beyond the comfort of the middle ground and to embrace a polarised approach that honours the unpredictable nature of markets and geopolitics. Metals, far from being niche or ornamental holdings, emerge as indispensable components of a portfolio designed not only to grow but, crucially, to survive.

Each paragraph here contributes to a layered understanding—linking theoretical frameworks, empirical evidence, practical implementation, and philosophical reflection. Readers are guided toward appreciating how gold and silver function within a barbell strategy not merely as assets but as foundational pillars of prudent, resilient wealth stewardship.

Beyond Percentages: How Much Metal Is Enough? –

The oft-cited rule of allocating five to ten per cent of one's portfolio to precious metals has become a comfortable mantra for many investors seeking diversification. Yet, this conventional wisdom, while serving as a convenient starting point, rarely reflects the nuanced realities of individual circumstances, risk appetites, or broader economic environments. To regard metals merely as a fixed percentage within a generic asset allocation framework is to overlook their profound strategic, psychological, and philosophical roles in wealth preservation. Beyond arbitrary numbers, determining how much gold and silver is enough demands a personalised approach—one that integrates one's worldview, financial objectives, risk tolerance, and the evolving dynamics of global markets.

At the heart of this personalised strategy lies an acknowledgement of metals as more than passive hedges. Unlike equities or bonds, which often derive their value from earnings or creditworthiness, precious metals possess intrinsic worth grounded in their physicality and historical trust. This foundational difference elevates the question from "What percentage of my portfolio should be in metals?" to "What role do metals play in safeguarding my unique conception of security?" For some, metals may function as a bulwark against systemic collapse, warranting a substantial allocation that reflects a deep-seated scepticism of fiat currencies and financial institutions. For others, metals serve as a tactical hedge against inflation or geopolitical turmoil, meriting a more modest position integrated into a broader risk mitigation scheme.

Historical precedent offers instructive context but stops short of prescriptive clarity. During periods of severe economic dislocation—such as the hyperinflations of the 20th century or the recent financial crises—allocations to gold and silver that far exceed ten per cent proved prescient, shielding capital from currency debasement and market collapses. Conversely, in prolonged bull markets for equities, excessive metal holdings may have underperformed, tempting investors to abandon these safeguards prematurely. The key insight is that metals do not conform neatly to static percentages; their optimal share fluctuates in response to macroeconomic signals, personal risk thresholds, and even psychological comfort.

Incorporating metals into a portfolio, therefore, requires a dynamic framework that moves beyond rote percentages. This includes a deep self-assessment: How vulnerable is one's wealth to monetary policy shifts, inflationary pressures, or geopolitical shocks? What timeframe governs investment horizons and liquidity needs? And crucially, what emotional resilience does the investor possess to withstand the volatility that accompanies metals' episodic price movements? These questions underscore that "enough" is a moving target, influenced as much by personal philosophy as by market metrics.

Practically, many sophisticated investors adopt a tiered approach, blending baseline holdings with opportunistic increments. A core holding might approximate the classic five to ten per cent, providing a foundation of stability. Above this, tactical additions respond to risk signals—rising inflation, currency depreciation, or geopolitical unrest—allowing the portfolio to flex and adapt. This active management eschews the pitfalls of rigid adherence to static allocations and recognises the unique protective qualities metals offer during times of systemic uncertainty.

Moreover, the interplay between gold and silver within these allocations deserves attention. Silver's dual role as both an industrial commodity and a precious metal renders it more volatile but also more opportunistic for certain investors. Tailoring the mix between gold's stability and silver's cyclical potential further refines one's metal strategy, moving beyond broad-brush allocation towards precise calibration aligned with economic context and personal preferences.

It is also imperative to factor in practical considerations such as storage, liquidity, and transaction costs, which influence the effective utility of metal holdings. An investor with limited access to physical bullion or insufficient knowledge of secure storage options may need to temper allocations or incorporate digital or trust-based products judiciously. Such operational realities can redefine what "enough" means in practice, as the value of metals is inseparable from one's ability to safeguard and mobilise them when needed.

Finally, embracing metals as a philosophy of wealth preservation challenges prevailing market dogma. It shifts the paradigm from seeking maximised short-term returns to prioritising survival and sovereignty over decades or generations. This perspective reframes "how much is enough" as a question of personal security and peace of mind, transcending formulaic asset allocation models. In doing so, it invites investors to integrate metals not as mere portfolio elements but as enduring expressions of their values and foresight.

By moving beyond generic allocation rules, investors cultivate bespoke metal strategies that are resilient, adaptable, and deeply aligned with their unique circumstances. This approach honours the complex, multifaceted nature of precious metals—anchoring portfolios against uncertainty while preserving flexibility to seize opportunity. It is through this lens of thoughtful personalization that the question of "how much metal is enough?" finds its most meaningful and actionable answers.

Rebalancing in a Fractured World –

The act of rebalancing a precious metals allocation is often perceived as a mechanical exercise—an adjustment in percentages to maintain a static portfolio mix. Yet, in the fractured world we inhabit today, where geopolitical upheavals, shifting economic paradigms, and technological disruptions redefine risk and opportunity with alarming rapidity, rebalancing demands a far more nuanced and dynamic approach. It is no longer sufficient to consider metals solely through the lens of market fluctuations; one must account for the broader currents shaping global stability, sovereignty, and financial resilience. Understanding when and how to recalibrate metal holdings becomes a sophisticated exercise in reading both economic indicators and the geopolitical environment, a practice that requires intellectual rigor and strategic foresight.

The traditional rebalancing paradigm, which advises returning to a fixed target allocation at predetermined intervals, assumes a degree of market predictability and institutional stability that is increasingly elusive. For instance, during times of acute inflation or currency devaluation, precious metals have historically served as a sanctuary, appreciating sharply even as equities and bonds falter. Conversely, periods of relative calm or market exuberance may see metals lag behind risk assets, tempting investors to reduce their exposure prematurely. The fractured world challenges the efficacy of rigid schedules; rebalancing must become responsive not just to asset price movements, but to evolving risk assessments shaped by factors as diverse as international conflicts, regulatory shifts, and emergent technologies like digital currencies.

A practical rebalancing framework thus integrates both quantitative metrics and qualitative judgments. Price-based triggers remain vital—when metals outperform significantly, trimming gains to lock in profits and maintain risk balance is prudent. However, equally important are signals from the geopolitical arena: escalating tensions, sanctions regimes, or political instability can presage structural risks that warrant increasing metal allocations regardless of short-term price behaviour. Similarly, developments in monetary policy—such as aggressive quantitative easing or tightening cycles—should influence rebalancing decisions, as they directly affect currency valuations and inflation expectations. This dual focus enables investors to balance tactical responsiveness with strategic vision.

Critical to effective rebalancing is the recognition that precious metals embody both financial instruments and philosophical anchors. The decision to increase metal holdings may stem not only from forecasted market trends but also from a conscious desire to preserve sovereignty and security amid systemic uncertainties. Conversely, reducing metal exposure can reflect confidence in institutional reforms or shifting personal risk appetites. Therefore, rebalancing transcends mere asset allocation; it becomes an ongoing dialogue between an investor's evolving worldview and the unfolding global landscape.

Real-world case studies underscore this complexity. Consider the surge in gold prices following the 2008 financial crisis, when rebalancing towards metals was not just profitable but existentially vital for many investors. Yet, in the subsequent decade of relative monetary stability and low inflation, maintaining high metal allocations proved costly for some, illustrating the risks of static allocations. More recently, geopolitical shocks—ranging from trade wars to armed conflicts—have triggered renewed metal accumulation, reflecting the shifting contours of global risk rather than mere price momentum. These examples illustrate that rebalancing in a fractured world demands vigilance, flexibility, and a broad perspective.

Another dimension involves the interplay between physical metals and digital or paper representations—ETFs, futures, and tokenized assets. Rebalancing strategies must factor in liquidity considerations and counterparty risks unique to these instruments. For example, in periods of market stress, physical metals may provide unmatched security, while digital assets offer liquidity advantages in normal times. Allocating and rebalancing across these modalities requires sophisticated judgement and an understanding of their distinct risk-return profiles.

Psychological discipline also plays a critical role. The fracturing of traditional economic and political certainties often heightens anxiety, which can lead to impulsive rebalancing decisions driven by fear or euphoria. Establishing a thoughtful, principles-based approach to rebalancing—rooted in clear investment objectives and a comprehensive understanding of risk—helps mitigate such emotional pitfalls. It encourages patience during volatility and confidence in long-term strategy, reinforcing metals' role as stabilizers rather than speculative gambles.

In practical terms, investors might develop flexible rebalancing thresholds rather than fixed percentages, allowing metal allocations to fluctuate within bands that reflect both market realities and risk assessments. Incorporating scenario analyses—considering, for example, the impact of escalating geopolitical tensions or sudden shifts in inflation—can inform when deviations from target allocations are warranted. Additionally, periodic reviews of one's overall risk landscape, including personal financial goals and broader economic conditions, ensure that rebalancing remains aligned with changing priorities.

Ultimately, rebalancing precious metals in a fractured world is a sophisticated act of stewardship. It calls for a balance between responsiveness and restraint, quantitative discipline and qualitative insight. By engaging deeply with both market data and the geopolitical context, investors can navigate complexity with greater clarity, preserving not only capital but the autonomy and security that metals uniquely provide. This approach elevates rebalancing from a technical task to a vital component of resilient wealth management in uncertain times.

Chapter 9
Gold ETFs, Mining Stocks & Sovereign Coins

In the intricate arena of precious metals investing, the divide between paper gold and physical ownership continues to provoke debate, confusion, and—if approached wisely—opportunity. Gold and silver have long stood as tangible symbols of security, yet the modern financialisation of these metals—through ETFs, mining equities, and sovereign coins—has layered additional dimensions onto their use. Each vehicle brings distinct advantages, risks, and strategic considerations. This chapter seeks to clarify these options, offering readers guidance on how to engage with the precious metals ecosystem in ways that reflect both their financial ambitions and philosophical stance on ownership.

At the core lies the distinction between paper gold and real, physical risk. Paper representations—ETFs, futures contracts, and certificates—allow investors to track price movements without the logistical burdens of storage or security. Convenience, however, carries its own price. Counterparty risk, potential liquidity constraints, and ambiguity over actual ownership can expose investors to vulnerabilities that tangible holdings avoid. This chapter examines when such instruments can enhance portfolio efficiency and when they may inadvertently mislead, emphasising the importance of understanding the invisible chains of trust underpinning paper positions.

Sovereign coins, by contrast, retain a unique blend of cultural significance, governmental assurance, and liquidity across global markets. Iconic issues—the American Gold Eagle, the British Britannia, the Canadian Maple Leaf—transcend their intrinsic metal content. They function not merely as bullion, but as legal tender with recognisable provenance, offering both practical and symbolic value. The chapter unpacks the advantages and caveats of these coins, framing them as investment tools that also carry deep historical and cultural resonance.

Mining equities introduce a further layer of complexity. Ownership here is not of metal itself but of operations extracting it from the earth—royalties, streaming companies, and mining stocks offer leveraged exposure to gold prices while introducing operational, geopolitical, and management risks. Understanding this landscape is crucial: mining instruments can complement physical holdings, enhancing returns for those willing to assume additional risk, or they can complicate a portfolio if deployed indiscriminately. Readers will explore how equities may function as both tactical opportunities and potential liabilities depending on timing, market conditions, and individual appetite for uncertainty.

Strategically, the modern investor benefits from "owning the system"—crafting a portfolio that marries physical metals with financial instruments to navigate between security and opportunity. In a world marked by fragmented markets, geopolitical turbulence, and experimental monetary policies, mastery over this spectrum of assets enables a balance of prudence and agility. This chapter emphasises portfolio design that accounts for both protection and participation, equipping investors to respond to evolving conditions with informed confidence.

Through case studies, empirical analysis, and reflective commentary, the chapter provides more than technical knowledge; it offers a conceptual framework for integrating ETFs, mining equities, and sovereign coins into a coherent metals strategy. Precious metals are thus repositioned—not as static holdings but as dynamic, multifaceted instruments whose value extends beyond the balance sheet. By the conclusion, readers will appreciate the nuanced interplay between convenience, tangibility, and strategy, gaining the insight necessary to harness metals as both anchors of stability and tools of strategic growth.

Paper Gold vs Real Risk –

The allure of gold has endured for millennia, symbolising wealth, stability, and trust. Yet in the modern financial ecosystem, the ways to own gold have diversified dramatically. Investors no longer must confine themselves to physical bars or coins; instead, paper gold products—such as Exchange-Traded Funds (ETFs), futures, and gold certificates—offer accessible, liquid, and ostensibly straightforward exposure to the precious metal. However, this apparent simplicity masks a complex and often misunderstood reality: owning paper gold is fundamentally different from holding physical metal. Recognising this distinction is crucial for investors who seek security, liquidity, and genuine protection against systemic risks.

At its core, paper gold represents a claim on gold, rather than possession of the metal itself. When an investor buys shares in a gold ETF or holds gold futures contracts, they are purchasing rights or promises contingent on the performance or backing of the issuer or custodian. This arrangement introduces counterparty risk—the risk that the party guaranteeing the gold will default or fail to deliver. In contrast, physical gold ownership confers direct control over an asset that is impervious to digital or institutional failure. This distinction is not merely academic; it has real implications during periods of financial distress, regulatory intervention, or market dislocation.

A critical example of this divergence emerged during the 2008 global financial crisis. While gold ETFs gained in popularity as convenient investment vehicles, several funds experienced liquidity strains, leading to spreads widening and concerns about the actual gold backing the shares. Meanwhile, physical gold holders reported challenges in selling at premium prices but retained the assurance of tangible assets immune to institutional insolvency. This episode underscores that paper gold can deliver price exposure but may not provide the protective qualities traditionally associated with metal ownership.

Yet paper gold is not inherently a trap. It serves a purpose within diversified portfolios, offering ease of transaction, cost efficiency, and immediate market access. Institutional investors, for example, rely on ETFs to efficiently allocate assets and hedge risks. Similarly, retail investors can benefit from paper gold when seeking incremental exposure without the complications of storage, security, and insurance. The key lies in discerning the suitability of paper gold relative to one's investment horizon, risk tolerance, and intent—whether speculative or preservative.

Investors must also scrutinise the terms underpinning paper gold products. Not all ETFs are created equal: some maintain full physical backing with segregated vaults, while others use pooled gold, increasing the risk of shortfalls in a crisis. Futures contracts, by their nature, are leveraged instruments that may amplify gains and losses, distancing the holder further from actual metal. Understanding these nuances demands critical examination beyond headline returns or market sentiment.

A further complexity arises from regulatory frameworks and market infrastructure. In jurisdictions where custodianship laws lack clarity or enforcement is weak, holders of paper gold might find their claims subordinate to creditors in bankruptcy scenarios. Conversely, physical gold stored in sovereign vaults or private facilities offers a degree of legal protection and sovereignty that paper gold cannot replicate. This legal landscape necessitates that investors view ownership not only as a financial transaction but as an exercise in risk assessment and jurisdictional prudence.

The psychology of ownership further complicates this equation. The tactile reassurance of holding a gold coin or bar appeals to deep-seated instincts about security and permanence. Paper gold, while functionally valuable, often fails to satisfy this psychological dimension, potentially leading to behavioural biases during market turmoil—panic selling or loss aversion that may not align with long-term goals.

Navigating these challenges requires a balanced approach. For investors prioritising liquidity and portfolio flexibility, a calibrated allocation to paper gold can complement physical holdings. For those focused on preserving capital through turbulent times, direct possession of metals remains paramount. The decision matrix involves evaluating the interplay of cost, convenience, risk, and control—eschewing one-size-fits-all prescriptions in favour of bespoke strategies attuned to individual circumstances.

Emerging technologies and market innovations continue to blur the boundaries between paper and physical gold. Tokenised gold on blockchain platforms promises transparent, real-time verification of physical backing, potentially reducing counterparty risk. Yet these developments are nascent and introduce new regulatory and cybersecurity considerations. Investors must remain vigilant, recognising that the evolution of gold ownership models carries both promise and peril.

Ultimately, distinguishing paper gold from real risk is a matter of philosophical as well as practical significance. It challenges investors to interrogate the nature of value, trust, and security in an increasingly abstracted financial world. It compels a reevaluation of what it means to "own" an asset and how that ownership translates into resilience against economic upheaval.

Understanding these dimensions equips investors not only to choose wisely among gold products but to integrate precious metals into a coherent framework of wealth preservation. By appreciating the limits and strengths of paper gold relative to physical possession, they can craft strategies that withstand the tests of time, market shocks, and the unpredictable dynamics of global finance.

This chapter invites readers to engage deeply with these issues, offering insight that transcends mere market speculation to embrace a richer conception of investment as stewardship—balancing liquidity with solidity, convenience with sovereignty, and abstract exposure with tangible security. It is an essential exploration for anyone seeking to navigate the modern gold market with wisdom, foresight, and conviction.

The Story Behind the Coin: Gold Eagles, Britannias, and Beyond –

The sovereign gold coin has long occupied a unique niche at the intersection of culture, finance, and national identity. Unlike generic bullion bars or anonymous gold held in vaults, these coins carry stories—of heritage, legal authority, and tangible liquidity—that imbue them with meaning beyond their intrinsic metal value. From the American Gold Eagle to the British Britannia, sovereign coins encapsulate centuries of tradition while serving as modern instruments for preserving wealth. Understanding their multifaceted role is essential for investors seeking not just gold, but the assurance that comes with official provenance and cultural resonance.

The appeal of sovereign coins begins with their cultural symbolism. These coins are emissaries of national pride and craftsmanship, often bearing designs that celebrate a country's history, mythology, or natural wonders. For instance, the American Gold Eagle prominently features Lady Liberty and a family of eagles—symbols rooted in the nation's founding ideals—while the Britannia's iconography draws on Roman Britain's emblem of strength and peace. This artistry does more than decorate; it conveys authenticity and reassures owners that their coins carry a heritage backed by the issuing state. The emotional connection forged by such symbolism often transcends the purely transactional nature of metal investment, offering holders a narrative that enriches the metal's value.

Legally, sovereign coins benefit from government backing that distinguishes them from private mint products or generic bullion. Issued and guaranteed by national mints or central banks, these coins typically hold legal tender status, meaning they are officially recognised as currency within their jurisdictions—even if their face value is far below their metal worth. This legal status enhances liquidity, making sovereign coins readily acceptable in secondary markets worldwide and simplifying processes such as customs clearance and valuation. For example, the Canadian Gold Maple Leaf, produced by the Royal Canadian Mint, is renowned not only for its high purity but also for the trust conferred by its government guarantee. Such legal frameworks reduce counterparty risk and provide owners with an assurance that their coins are genuine and redeemable.

Liquidity is a paramount consideration for investors, and sovereign coins excel in this regard. Their recognisable designs and established reputations facilitate quick identification and authentication, critical factors when time and trust are scarce commodities. Dealers and collectors across global markets often accept these coins without hesitation, allowing for smoother transactions compared to lesser-known private mint products. The market's familiarity with sovereign coins translates into narrower bid-ask spreads and greater price transparency, both vital for investors needing to convert their holdings efficiently. Moreover, sovereign coins are generally exempt or subject to favourable tax treatments in many countries, further enhancing their attractiveness as liquid assets.

However, sovereign coins are not without complexities. The premium over spot gold prices—the additional cost reflecting minting, distribution, and branding—can vary significantly. Investors must discern when these premiums are justified by the coin's cultural, legal, and liquidity advantages and when they represent speculative markups. For instance, certain limited-edition or commemorative issues command higher premiums driven by collector demand rather than metal content, introducing a different risk profile. Balancing these factors requires a nuanced understanding of market dynamics and personal investment objectives.

Contrasting sovereign coins with other forms of gold ownership highlights their distinctive place in a portfolio. Unlike ETFs or futures, sovereign coins are physical assets that the owner can hold, store, or gift without reliance on intermediaries. Unlike bullion bars, their standardised size and official status often simplify valuation and ease of trade. Furthermore, their cultural resonance provides a form of psychological security, affirming ownership in a manner that purely financial instruments cannot replicate. This blend of tangible and intangible value makes sovereign coins appealing for investors seeking a comprehensive relationship with their precious metals.

The global landscape of sovereign coin issuance also reflects geopolitical and economic considerations. Nations with robust minting traditions and stable governance tend to produce the most trusted coins, while emerging markets may offer coins with attractive premiums but heightened risks. Political shifts, changes in tax policy, or alterations in minting standards can influence the desirability and reliability of these coins, underscoring the need for ongoing vigilance and market knowledge. In this sense, sovereign coins are not static assets but participants in a dynamic interplay of national policy, cultural identity, and global economics.

Digital technology and modern minting innovations further enrich the sovereign coin narrative. High-definition engraving, security features such as micro-etching and holograms, and blockchain-based provenance tracking enhance authenticity and deter counterfeiting. These advancements reinforce trust and open new avenues for collectors and investors alike. Yet they also raise questions about balancing tradition with innovation—whether the value of a sovereign coin lies solely in its metal content and state guarantee or also in its evolving technological safeguards.

In navigating the sovereign coin market, the discerning investor must balance appreciation of cultural and legal significance with pragmatic financial assessment. Each coin carries a layered story, entwined with the history of a nation and the evolving demands of a global marketplace. Appreciating this complexity transforms the act of acquiring sovereign coins from a mere transaction into a deliberate engagement with heritage, legality, and liquidity.

This exploration reveals that sovereign gold coins represent more than metal—they are vessels of meaning and trust, blending heritage with financial utility. For those seeking to integrate gold into a resilient and meaningful portfolio, understanding these coins' multifaceted roles offers invaluable guidance. It is an invitation to hold not just an asset, but a story—one that enriches the investor's connection to gold as both a material and cultural cornerstone.

Mining Stocks: Leveraged Gold or a Different Beast? –

Gold mining stocks, royalties, and streaming companies represent a complex yet potentially rewarding frontier in precious metals investing—one that often defies simplistic categorisation as mere "leveraged gold." Understanding these instruments demands a nuanced grasp of their distinct characteristics, inherent risks, and strategic roles within a diversified portfolio. Unlike direct ownership of physical gold, investing in mining equities introduces layers of operational, geopolitical, and financial variables, while royalty and streaming companies offer exposure with a different risk-reward profile. For the discerning investor, mastering these distinctions is crucial to aligning metal-related equities with personal goals and risk tolerance.

At first glance, gold mining stocks might appear as straightforward proxies for the metal price. Their values typically exhibit a leveraged relationship with gold, meaning their price movements can exceed those of bullion. When gold prices rise, mining shares often surge disproportionately, reflecting improved profit margins and investor optimism. Conversely, they can fall more sharply during downturns. However, treating mining stocks solely as "leveraged gold" overlooks vital complexities. Mining companies are operational enterprises subject to a range of internal and external pressures—from geological challenges and environmental regulations to labour disputes and capital expenditure demands—that can significantly affect their performance independent of gold prices.

Royalty and streaming companies constitute a distinct subset of the mining ecosystem. Rather than operating mines, these firms provide upfront capital to mining companies in exchange for a percentage of future production or revenue, often at predetermined prices. This business model reduces operational risk and capital intensity, offering a more stable income stream and typically lower volatility than traditional mining stocks. For instance, companies like Franco-Nevada and Wheaton Precious Metals have become favourites among investors seeking gold exposure with a smoother risk profile. Yet, these firms are not immune to market shifts; their fortunes depend on the success and longevity of the mines they finance, and contractual terms can influence profitability.

Investors must consider the multifaceted risk landscape associated with mining equities. Unlike physical gold, whose intrinsic value endures, mining stocks are exposed to corporate governance quality, management expertise, and capital structure decisions. Political risk looms large as well; mines often operate in jurisdictions where regulatory frameworks can shift abruptly, sometimes jeopardising operations or ownership rights. Environmental and social governance (ESG) factors are increasingly critical, affecting both company reputation and regulatory compliance. The recent surge in ESG-focused investing underscores that mining companies with poor sustainability practices may face higher financing costs or exclusion from certain investment pools, impacting share performance.

The valuation of mining stocks also incorporates growth expectations, as companies continually explore new deposits and develop projects. This speculative element introduces a dimension not present in bullion ownership. An exploration success can propel a junior miner's stock price exponentially, while failures may lead to steep losses. Larger, established producers offer more stability but are often priced for their steady cash flows and dividends, sometimes at the cost of outsized gains. Here, personal risk tolerance and investment horizon become pivotal. Aggressive investors might allocate to juniors for growth potential, while conservative ones may prefer majors or royalty firms for resilience and income.

A critical tension exists between the appeal of mining stocks' leverage and the need for diversification within the sector. Not all gold miners behave alike; geographic concentration, mine lifecycle stages, and operational focus vary considerably. Some companies operate in politically stable regions with mature mines, while others pursue high-risk, high-reward projects in frontier territories. Sector-specific diversification can mitigate idiosyncratic risks but requires diligent research and portfolio monitoring. This complexity contrasts with the simplicity of physical gold, which is universally recognised and unencumbered by operational risks.

Integrating mining equities into an overall precious metals strategy involves discerning their appropriate role—whether as complements to physical holdings or as vehicles for tactical market plays. Mining stocks can enhance portfolio returns during bull markets due to their leveraged nature but should be balanced against the stability of bullion and coins. Royalty and streaming companies, with their hybrid risk profiles, serve as attractive intermediaries offering exposure with moderated volatility. Understanding these gradations allows investors to tailor allocations dynamically, responding to market conditions and personal objectives.

Ethical considerations are inseparable from mining investments. The mining industry faces scrutiny over environmental degradation, labour practices, and community relations. Increasingly, investors demand transparency and responsibility, influencing company policies and, by extension, share valuations. Engaging with these issues reflects a broader trend in responsible investing, underscoring that mining stocks are not merely financial instruments but entities embedded within social and ecological contexts. For some investors, aligning metal-related equities with personal values is as important as financial metrics.

Market timing and macroeconomic factors also weigh heavily. Mining stocks tend to outperform physical gold during periods of rising inflation and currency depreciation but may underperform during times of economic contraction or equity market turmoil. Additionally, supply-demand dynamics in the gold market, technological advances in mining, and shifts in central bank policies can create divergent performance paths for miners versus bullion. Astute investors monitor these indicators to anticipate inflection points and adjust exposure accordingly, recognising that mining equities require active oversight distinct from passive bullion ownership.

Finally, liquidity considerations influence the choice of mining-related investments. Major mining companies and large royalty firms trade on established exchanges with ample volume, facilitating entry and exit. Junior miners, while offering growth potential, often suffer from thin trading and price volatility, raising execution risks. Investors must assess their liquidity needs, willingness to tolerate price swings, and capacity for thorough due diligence when selecting mining stocks.

This examination reveals that gold mining stocks, royalties, and streaming companies are not monolithic "leveraged gold" but varied instruments with unique risk-return profiles and strategic functions. Approaching them with an informed, critical mindset enables investors to harness their opportunities while mitigating inherent challenges. Aligning these equities with individual goals and risk tolerance transforms metal investment from simple exposure to a sophisticated, purposeful endeavour.

Owning the System, Not Just the Metal –

Owning gold today is no longer confined to holding physical bars or coins; it has evolved into a multifaceted engagement with an intricate financial ecosystem. Understanding how to *own the system*, rather than just the metal itself, is paramount for investors who seek to harness the full strategic potential of gold-related instruments. This approach transcends traditional notions of gold as a mere store of value and positions it as a dynamic tool that can be wielded both offensively and defensively across varying market environments. For the discerning investor, mastering these instruments means recognising the interplay between bullion, derivatives, mining equities, ETFs, and alternative financial products—each offering distinct advantages and risks aligned with diverse investment objectives.

The distinction between owning physical gold and participating in the broader gold ecosystem is critical. Physical gold provides tangible security—an immutable asset that exists independently of counterparties. Yet, in a world driven by speed, liquidity, and market complexity, relying solely on physical possession may constrain an investor's ability to react to rapidly shifting economic conditions. Instruments such as gold futures, options, exchange-traded funds (ETFs), and mining stocks allow investors to *play offense*, seeking gains through leveraged exposure, arbitrage opportunities, or tactical rebalancing. Conversely, gold's enduring reputation as a safe haven enables these instruments to serve defensive purposes—acting as hedges against inflation, currency debasement, or geopolitical uncertainty. To leverage this duality requires a sophisticated understanding of each vehicle's mechanics and the macroeconomic signals that dictate their optimal use.

Gold ETFs, for example, represent a widely accessible gateway into the metal's market dynamics. By owning shares in an ETF, investors can gain exposure to gold's price movements without the logistical challenges of physical storage and security. These funds facilitate rapid entry and exit, essential for tactical manoeuvres amid volatile markets. However, ETF ownership is essentially a claim on gold held by custodians, subject to counterparty and operational risks. This nuance highlights a recurring tension within gold investing: the trade-off between liquidity and sovereignty. Yet, ETFs are invaluable in portfolio management, enabling dynamic allocation shifts that reflect evolving market narratives, especially during episodes of heightened uncertainty.

Derivatives, including futures and options, amplify this tactical flexibility. Futures contracts allow investors to lock in prices, hedge existing exposures, or speculate on directional moves without immediate capital outlay on physical gold. Options introduce optionality, providing asymmetric payoff profiles that can protect downside risk while maintaining upside potential. The sophistication of these instruments empowers market participants to architect complex strategies—such as collars, spreads, and straddles—that can defend portfolios in downturns or capitalise on emerging trends. Yet, these vehicles demand rigorous risk management and expertise, as missteps can magnify losses or incur significant margin calls, underscoring the importance of disciplined, informed engagement.

Mining stocks and royalty companies add another layer to owning the gold system. While mining equities exhibit higher volatility and operational risks compared to bullion, they offer leveraged participation in the gold price and potential for dividends and capital appreciation. Moreover, mining companies often react not only to gold prices but also to broader commodity cycles, geopolitical risks, and management efficacy. Royalty and streaming firms provide a hybrid exposure, earning income through contractual agreements without the direct burden of mining operations. Their distinct risk profiles and cash flow characteristics allow investors to fine-tune exposure to gold's economic ecosystem beyond physical ownership.

Integral to this ecosystem is an appreciation of gold's role as an insurance asset in diversified portfolios. Holding physical gold or its financial proxies equips investors to mitigate systemic shocks—whether from inflationary surges, currency devaluations, or financial crises. Owning the system means blending physical holdings with liquid instruments, creating a barbell strategy that balances permanence and agility. This synthesis permits investors to *defend* wealth during crises through physical security while *offensively* pursuing growth or arbitrage with paper-based exposures. For example, during periods of geopolitical tension or monetary instability, physical gold serves as an unassailable anchor, whereas ETFs and futures can be deployed to tactically amplify gains or hedge against anticipated shifts.

Moreover, the evolution of digital assets has introduced tokenised gold products, offering yet another dimension of participation. While these innovations promise unprecedented liquidity and fractional ownership, they reintroduce concerns around custodial risk, regulatory oversight, and market fragmentation. Here again, owning the system means weighing convenience against sovereignty and selecting instruments that align with one's philosophical and practical priorities. Pragmatic investors scrutinise not only the underlying asset but also the infrastructure and governance models supporting these products.

Navigating this complex terrain also demands an acute sensitivity to market context and timing. Gold-related instruments react variably depending on macroeconomic conditions, interest rate cycles, and investor sentiment. For instance, rising real interest rates often weigh on gold prices, impacting mining stocks disproportionately due to their capital costs and operational leverage. Conversely, inflationary spikes may trigger rapid reallocations into physical bullion and ETFs, reflecting heightened risk aversion. Understanding these differentiated responses enables investors to calibrate their system-wide gold exposure dynamically, shifting allocations among instruments to optimise performance and risk management.

In embracing this holistic ownership approach, investors must also confront the challenge of behavioural discipline. The availability of diverse gold instruments can tempt reactive, emotionally driven decisions, particularly during market turbulence. Successful ownership of the system requires a clear strategic framework, underpinned by long-term objectives, risk tolerance, and systematic evaluation. This mindset transforms gold from a static asset into an active component of portfolio strategy—one that is continually assessed and recalibrated in response to evolving financial and geopolitical landscapes.

Ultimately, *owning the system* is a call for intellectual rigor and practical sophistication. It urges investors to transcend simplistic asset classifications and engage deeply with the full spectrum of gold-related opportunities. This integrated perspective not only enhances potential returns but also fortifies resilience, offering a nuanced toolkit for both offence and defence. The mastery of gold's financial ecosystem empowers investors to navigate complexity with confidence, harnessing the metal's enduring value in multifarious ways that reflect both market realities and personal conviction.

Chapter 10
Wealth Preservation in an Age of Soft Money

In today's era of "soft money"—where expansive monetary policies, mounting debt, and the persistent spectre of inflation define the financial landscape—the imperative of wealth preservation has never felt more pressing or more intricate. At its essence, this chapter confronts a fundamental reality: inflation is not an abstract number but a quiet, relentless erosion of purchasing power, gradually nibbling away at the true value of money and assets. It seldom makes headlines, yet it quietly shapes the anxieties of those intent on safeguarding their wealth. Gold and silver, with their enduring intrinsic properties, have historically offered a bulwark against this slow decay, providing a tangible refuge in an otherwise intangible financial world.

Standard economic indicators—GDP, the Consumer Price Index, and similar benchmarks—are widely invoked to measure economic health and inflation, yet they can mislead as much as they inform. The so-called "tyranny of numbers" arises from methodological constraints, political influence, and the challenge of distilling complex, dynamic economies into simplified indices. GDP growth, for example, may conceal widening inequality or asset bubbles, while CPI adjustments frequently understate the real costs endured by households, particularly in essentials such as food, energy, and housing. This chapter encourages readers to look beyond conventional statistics, revealing the subtle yet pervasive ways in which official metrics can diverge from lived economic reality—a divergence critical to anyone seeking genuine wealth preservation.

Beyond guarding nominal value, precious metals preserve optionality. When fiat systems falter—through devaluation, capital controls, or systemic shocks—gold and silver offer mobility, privacy, and transactional freedom that paper assets cannot replicate. They serve as instruments of sovereignty, allowing holders to maintain choices in circumstances where conventional investments may become illiquid, confiscated, or heavily devalued. This chapter explores the philosophical dimension of metals as more than commodities; they are strategic reserves of freedom, a hedge against the limitations imposed by failing financial infrastructures and digital oversight.

Finally, wealth itself is reframed not as consumption or status but as enduring capacity. The principle of "choosing legacy over luxury" shifts the lens from transient spending power to long-term influence, advocating for wealth that secures future possibilities rather than ephemeral pleasures. Metals, with a history spanning millennia as repositories of value, naturally anchor this pursuit. Readers are invited to consider the ethical and practical dimensions of preserving assets that endure, reflecting on what it truly means to leave a legacy in a world where the purchasing power of currency is constantly under siege.

Throughout this discussion, the chapter equips readers with a sophisticated understanding of wealth preservation: how to navigate misleading economic indicators, safeguard purchasing power, and leverage the intrinsic strengths of gold and silver. It offers an intellectually rigorous guide, blending practical strategy with philosophical insight, for those determined not merely to survive the vicissitudes of soft money but to secure freedom, resilience, and lasting influence.

Inflation as Erosion: The Silent Thief

Inflation, often discussed in abstract terms or dismissed as a mere economic footnote, operates as a relentless force that quietly undermines the real value of money and wealth. It is not an abrupt event but a steady, unyielding process—an erosion that chips away at purchasing power with insidious subtlety. Unlike theft or loss that is immediate and visible, inflation's damage accumulates over time, making it easy to overlook until its effects become undeniable. For individuals and institutions alike, recognising inflation as this "silent thief" is crucial for preserving the integrity of wealth in a world where currency debasement is a recurring theme rather than an anomaly.

At its core, inflation measures the rate at which the general level of prices for goods and services rises, thereby decreasing the value of currency. What this means in practical terms is that each unit of money buys fewer goods and services than before. Historical examples highlight the devastating impact of unchecked inflation. The Weimar Republic's hyperinflation in the early 1920s obliterated savings, transforming once-stable wealth into worthless paper almost overnight. More recent episodes, such as Zimbabwe's crisis in the late 2000s or Venezuela's ongoing economic collapse, echo similar themes: currency collapse leading to societal upheaval and the erosion of trust in fiat systems. Yet even moderate inflation, often tolerated or overlooked in developed economies, silently diminishes wealth, penalising savers and those on fixed incomes while rewarding debtors and speculative interests.

This erosion is particularly pernicious because it affects different groups unevenly and often contradicts popular perceptions of economic growth and prosperity. While headline GDP figures might suggest an expanding economy, the reality for many is shrinking purchasing power, rising living costs, and increased financial insecurity. Inflation acts as a regressive tax, disproportionately burdening the most vulnerable, those without access to inflation-protected assets or the means to hedge against rising prices. This discrepancy challenges the often-sanitised narratives around inflation, underscoring its ethical dimensions and raising fundamental questions about economic justice and sustainability.

In this environment, precious metals—chiefly gold and silver—have demonstrated enduring value as defensive terrain against inflation's erosion. Their historical role as stores of value is not merely symbolic but rooted in tangible economic functions. Unlike fiat currency, gold and silver cannot be created at will by central banks; their scarcity and physical permanence confer intrinsic worth. When inflation erodes paper money, metals have consistently preserved purchasing power, offering a reliable hedge that transcends borders and political regimes. This protective quality has been affirmed repeatedly across centuries, from the Roman Empire's coinage reforms to modern portfolio strategies aimed at inflation-proofing wealth.

Moreover, the relationship between metals and inflation is neither mechanical nor guaranteed but complex and nuanced. Metals serve as both a barometer and a refuge—prices tend to rise in anticipation of inflationary pressures as investors seek safe havens, yet metals also react to broader macroeconomic forces such as interest rates, geopolitical tensions, and currency fluctuations. Understanding these dynamics is essential for those seeking to deploy metals effectively within a broader wealth preservation strategy. It involves discerning when metals offer genuine protection and when market sentiment or speculative excess may distort their value.

This chapter delves deeply into inflation's role as a covert eroder of value and explores how metals function as a bulwark against this threat. Through historical analysis, empirical data, and critical evaluation of monetary policies, it equips readers with the intellectual tools to appreciate why metals remain vital in an age of persistent monetary expansion. It challenges complacency toward inflation, urging readers to recognise it as a fundamental financial reality rather than an abstract concept. More importantly, it offers practical insights into leveraging metals not just as passive hedges but as active components of a resilient financial armoury, adaptable to shifting economic landscapes.

Examining real-world applications, the chapter presents case studies of investors and institutions who have successfully navigated inflationary environments by integrating metals into diversified portfolios. It also addresses common misconceptions that metals are merely speculative or outdated relics, contrasting these views with rigorous analysis of metals' unique capacity to retain real value. Ethical reflections underscore the societal implications of inflation, prompting readers to consider the broader consequences of monetary policy and the role of personal responsibility in wealth stewardship.

Ultimately, this discussion reframes inflation from a statistical annoyance into a profound challenge demanding thoughtful response. Metals emerge not simply as commodities or investments but as strategic tools that defend the foundational principle of wealth—the ability to preserve and exercise purchasing power over time. By engaging with inflation as a silent thief, readers are invited to cultivate a proactive stance, understanding that safeguarding wealth requires vigilance, knowledge, and a commitment to durable value in an uncertain monetary world.

The Tyranny of Numbers: Why GDP and CPI Lie

Gross Domestic Product (GDP) and the Consumer Price Index (CPI) are the twin pillars of modern economic measurement, cited ubiquitously in policy debates, financial analyses, and media reports. Yet, beneath their veneer of objectivity lies a troubling reality: these figures often mislead more than they inform. Far from offering a transparent window into economic health and living standards, GDP and CPI can distort our understanding of real value, perpetuating flawed narratives that shape decisions at every level—from governments to individual investors. This distortion is not incidental but structurally embedded within the methodologies and incentives that drive these metrics, revealing the profound limitations of relying solely on such aggregated numbers to navigate complex economic realities.

GDP, long regarded as the definitive measure of a nation's economic performance, quantifies the total monetary value of all goods and services produced within a country over a specified period. Its simplicity and comparability have secured its central place in economics, yet its conceptual foundations mask critical shortcomings. GDP measures activity, not wellbeing; it counts all economic transactions, including those that may be socially or environmentally harmful, while ignoring the quality, distribution, or sustainability of that activity. For example, natural disasters that trigger costly rebuilding efforts paradoxically increase GDP, despite representing a loss in real wealth and human suffering. Similarly, GDP does not account for income inequality, leaving unanswered how growth is experienced across different societal strata.

The CPI, designed to track changes in consumer prices and thus inflation, suffers from its own methodological constraints. Constructed as a weighted basket of goods and services presumed representative of the "average" consumer's expenditure, the CPI aims to capture price movements over time. Yet the reality of consumer behaviour, technological change, and product substitution complicates this picture. Adjustments like hedonic quality corrections, which account for improvements in product features, can mask actual cost increases faced by consumers. The choice and weighting of basket items, often influenced by political and bureaucratic considerations, further undermine CPI's claim to accuracy. As a result, official inflation rates may understate the cost pressures felt by ordinary households, especially in essentials like housing, healthcare, and education.

This discrepancy between official statistics and lived experience is not merely academic. It shapes monetary policy, wage negotiations, social security adjustments, and investment strategies—areas where misjudging real value can have severe consequences. Central banks, reliant on GDP growth and CPI inflation targets, may pursue policies that fail to address structural economic issues, exacerbate asset bubbles, or overlook growing financial precarity. For the individual investor or saver, a misread inflation figure can erode purchasing power silently, while the illusion of steady GDP growth might encourage complacency in portfolio risk management.

Moreover, GDP and CPI do not adequately capture the qualitative dimensions of economic life, such as environmental degradation, resource depletion, and social capital erosion. These "externalities" have profound long-term impacts but remain largely invisible within traditional accounting frameworks. Consequently, decisions based on these numbers risk prioritising short-term output over sustainable prosperity, setting the stage for economic and ecological crises.

This chapter explores these challenges with a critical eye, unpacking the construction, limitations, and implications of GDP and CPI. Through historical context and contemporary case studies, it reveals how these indicators have evolved alongside political and economic agendas, often serving as tools for legitimising particular narratives rather than objective measures. It engages with alternative frameworks—such as the Genuine Progress Indicator (GPI), Human Development Index (HDI), and measures of economic wellbeing—that attempt to correct the blind spots of conventional metrics. These alternatives underscore the necessity of adopting a more nuanced, multidimensional approach to assessing economic health and value.

Importantly, the chapter does not dismiss GDP and CPI outright but advocates for informed scepticism and contextual interpretation. It encourages readers to recognise these numbers as proxies subject to manipulation and misunderstanding rather than absolute truths. This perspective equips professionals and thoughtful investors with a more robust framework for decision-making—one that integrates qualitative insights, real-world observations, and an awareness of underlying economic complexities.

Ethical considerations permeate this analysis, inviting reflection on the consequences of blind reliance on flawed data. How does the misrepresentation of economic reality affect policy equity, intergenerational justice, and democratic accountability? What responsibilities do economists, policymakers, and investors bear in communicating and responding to these distortions? Addressing these questions highlights the broader societal stakes embedded in seemingly technical debates over numbers.

Ultimately, this chapter serves as a call to intellectual rigor and practical wisdom. It challenges readers to move beyond simplistic acceptance of headline figures and to cultivate a critical understanding of economic indicators as part of a larger epistemological and ethical landscape. By doing so, it deepens the reader's capacity to discern real value amid numerical noise and to navigate the economic terrain with clarity and confidence.

Preserving Optionality: What Gold Buys When Nothing Else Works

In a world defined by accelerating uncertainty—geopolitical upheavals, systemic financial shocks, and sweeping technological transformations—the true value of gold transcends its immediate market price. Gold functions as a unique form of *optional wealth*: a reserve of liquidity, privacy, and leverage that preserves future choices precisely when conventional systems falter. This capacity to safeguard *optionality*—the freedom to act decisively in moments of crisis or transition—distinguishes gold from other assets that depend on the stability and trustworthiness of intermediaries, regulatory frameworks, or digital infrastructure. Far beyond a mere store of value, gold embodies the preservation of autonomy itself in the face of systemic failure.

The concept of optionality, rooted in financial theory yet applicable in broader contexts, refers to the value inherent in having the right—but not the obligation—to make a decision under uncertain conditions. While equities and bonds offer expected returns contingent on economic growth and policy, gold's enduring nature and intrinsic worth provide an escape hatch, a contingency plan when traditional assets lose viability. This dynamic is neither theoretical nor abstract. Throughout history—from hyperinflations in Weimar Germany and Zimbabwe to banking freezes in Cyprus and Argentina—gold has repeatedly emerged as the asset that preserves *real choice* when currencies collapse, capital controls tighten, or political turmoil disrupts markets.

One dimension of this optionality is *mobility*. Physical gold, unlike many financial assets, is transportable and accepted across borders with minimal friction. In times when capital restrictions or asset freezes are imposed, the ability to physically carry or transfer wealth can determine survival and freedom. The stories of refugees, dissidents, and expatriates who have relied on portable precious metals to rebuild lives underscore gold's unique portability advantage. This attribute is increasingly relevant today as governments globally expand regulatory reach over capital flows and digital transactions, raising questions about the inviolability of financial privacy and sovereignty.

Closely linked to mobility is *privacy*, a feature gold inherently preserves due to its tangible, bearer form. Unlike bank accounts or digital currencies, which leave comprehensive transactional footprints accessible to institutions and potentially governments, gold ownership is not recorded in centralised ledgers. This anonymity safeguards not only wealth but also personal liberty—critical when political regimes change abruptly or when surveillance intensifies. The growing concerns over data privacy and financial censorship highlight gold's role as a hedge against intrusive control mechanisms. However, this privacy is neither absolute nor costless; it requires responsible custodianship and prudent risk assessment.

The third facet—*leverage*—relates to gold's capacity to secure credit or act as collateral in periods when conventional credit channels constrict. Historical episodes, such as the 2008 financial crisis, demonstrated how the erosion of trust in financial institutions leads to tightened lending and diminished liquidity. Gold, owing to its universal acceptance and stable intrinsic value, can serve as a reliable form of collateral, enabling access to credit when other assets become illiquid or devalued. This leverage extends beyond individual investors to nations and corporations that deploy gold reserves to underpin financial stability or monetary credibility.

Nevertheless, preserving optionality through gold demands deliberate strategy and understanding of its limitations. The physicality that enables mobility and privacy also poses challenges of secure storage and verification. The liquidity of gold, while generally robust, depends on market conditions and can fluctuate markedly during crises. Moreover, the psychological dimension—gold's symbolic resonance as a refuge—can amplify both rational and irrational behaviours, influencing market dynamics unpredictably. Recognising these complexities is essential to avoid missteps such as overexposure, illiquidity traps, or security breaches.

The modern investor must therefore view gold not as a static asset class but as a *dynamic reserve of freedom*, integrated thoughtfully within a diversified framework that accounts for evolving risks and opportunities. This perspective aligns with philosophical and ethical considerations about wealth preservation: what is the purpose of holding wealth if it cannot protect agency or adapt to unforeseen disruptions? Gold, when rightly understood and managed, offers more than financial security—it preserves the *capacity to choose*, a principle that anchors human resilience in the face of volatility.

This article situates gold's role within the broader context of systemic fragility and individual empowerment. Through case studies of recent crises and analyses of emerging geopolitical and technological trends, it elucidates how gold's unique attributes safeguard optionality. It challenges conventional risk paradigms that equate wealth solely with growth and advocates for a recalibration towards *preserving flexibility and autonomy*. Ultimately, it aims to deepen the reader's appreciation of gold's irreplaceable function as the ultimate safeguard of future possibilities, offering insights that transcend mere portfolio construction to touch on the very essence of security and freedom.

Choosing Legacy Over Luxury

Wealth, in its most profound expression, transcends immediate gratification. It is not merely a measure of what one can spend today but a reflection of enduring capacity—the ability to influence, empower, and protect across generations. This reorientation from luxury to legacy challenges prevailing cultural narratives that equate wealth with conspicuous consumption and transient pleasures. Instead, it invites a deeper contemplation of what it means to *own* wealth in a manner that preserves not only financial assets but also values, opportunities, and stability for the future. This shift in perspective is critical in a world marked by rapid change, economic volatility, and complex intergenerational dynamics.

Understanding wealth as legacy begins by recognising its dual nature: it is both a resource for present use and a reservoir for future preservation. The tension between spending for immediate enjoyment and saving for long-term impact is not merely financial but existential. It asks what we prioritise—momentary indulgence or sustained influence. This dilemma is especially poignant in the context of precious metals, which have historically symbolised enduring value and security. Gold and silver, for example, embody *timelessness*; their physical permanence contrasts sharply with the fleeting nature of luxury goods, which depreciate or become obsolete. Thus, allocating wealth towards metals is not just an investment decision but a deliberate act of legacy-building.

The concept of legacy also encompasses the ethical dimension of wealth. It compels consideration of how resources can be deployed responsibly to support family, community, and broader societal goals. The choices made about wealth preservation reflect one's values and intentions. For instance, prioritising intergenerational transfer through trusts or foundations demonstrates a commitment to *sustaining influence* beyond one's lifetime. This approach guards against the erosion of wealth by impulsive spending or shortsighted decisions. It acknowledges the fragility of material success and the necessity of deliberate stewardship.

Practical strategies for choosing legacy over luxury demand discipline and foresight. They require setting clear objectives that differentiate between consumption and conservation. Creating a wealth plan that integrates physical assets, such as precious metals, with other holdings allows for flexibility while maintaining a core of durable value. Moreover, legacy-focused investors embrace education and engagement with heirs to cultivate financial literacy and shared responsibility. This cultural transmission ensures that the principles underpinning legacy endure alongside the assets themselves.

Case studies reveal the consequences of neglecting legacy in favour of luxury. Stories abound of fortunes dissipated within a generation due to lack of planning or disregard for enduring principles. Conversely, families who embed legacy in their wealth management often navigate economic upheavals with resilience. Their wealth becomes a platform for opportunities—funding education, entrepreneurial ventures, or philanthropy—that extend impact well beyond mere accumulation.

In rethinking wealth, it is essential to challenge reductionist views that frame financial success purely in terms of accumulation or consumption. Legacy demands a holistic understanding that incorporates emotional, cultural, and relational facets. It invites reflection on how wealth shapes identity, purpose, and social capital. Ultimately, choosing legacy over luxury redefines what it means to be truly wealthy: it is not what one owns in the present but what one preserves and passes on, ensuring that wealth remains a source of empowerment rather than fleeting pleasure.

This subchapter offers readers not only a theoretical framework but also actionable insights for cultivating a legacy mindset. It integrates financial principles with ethical reflection and practical guidance, encouraging a deliberate and values-driven approach to wealth management. By adopting this stance, readers position themselves to harness wealth's full potential—as a tool for enduring security, meaningful impact, and intergenerational connection—rather than succumbing to the ephemeral allure of luxury.

Conclusion
Holding What Matters

At the close of this examination of precious metals and wealth preservation, there emerges a quiet but profound invitation: to approach one's financial life not as a series of transactions, but as a considered practice rooted in clarity, permanence, and dignity. This final chapter moves beyond the mechanics of acquiring, storing, or selling gold and silver, encouraging readers to regard these metals not merely as assets, but as instruments of preparation—anchors in turbulent times and markers of mindful stewardship. Here, the journey converges on a philosophy of ownership that marries practical insight with enduring values, revealing how the tangible holdings in one's possession reflect and shape the intangible qualities of security, legacy, and agency.

The themes developed across earlier chapters coalesce here. Gold's historical resilience through economic upheavals has been traced; the nuanced tension between physical possession and digital representation dissected; the psychology of investment choices explored. Yet, the essence of "holding what matters" transcends mere portfolio optimisation or crisis hedging; it embodies a deliberate orientation towards wealth—balancing transience with tenacity, immediacy with foresight. This chapter invites readers to recalibrate their relationship with money, framing wealth as a canvas upon which identity, responsibility, and freedom are continuously inscribed.

At its core, precious metals represent more than financial instruments. They provide a tangible link to history, culture, and the material world, countering the intangibility and volatility that characterise modern finance. Gold and silver confer a sense of sovereignty over one's resources—a control often elusive within digital or fiat systems. Such sovereignty, however, is instrumental rather than purely symbolic; it cultivates resilience, the ability to withstand shocks, navigate uncertainty, and preserve optionality for future choices. In this light, metals become both symbol and substance of preparedness, aligning economic security with psychological equilibrium.

The practical ramifications of this stance are manifold. Readers are encouraged to infuse their wealth strategies with intentionality—deciding not merely what to hold, but why, when, and how. This includes considerations of storage, liquidity, diversification, and legacy planning, all framed within a commitment to sustainability and ethical stewardship. Real-world narratives illustrate these principles in action: families and individuals who, through thoughtful planning, navigated crises with composure, preserving both wealth and agency. Such examples underscore the transformative power of deliberate holding, converting inert metals into dynamic agents of enduring value.

Equally significant is the chapter's engagement with the ethical and societal dimensions of wealth. "Holding what matters" entails recognising the responsibilities inherent in possession—responsibilities extending beyond oneself to community and posterity. This perspective encourages readers to examine not only their financial aims, but also the values these goals express. Wealth, in this sense, becomes a vehicle for meaningful impact, whether through philanthropy, education, or intergenerational transfer. Precious metals thus act as conduits, linking present agency with future possibility, grounding abstract ideals in tangible reality.

The narrative maintains a tone that is both intellectually rigorous and accessible, blending analytical precision with the clarity of a seasoned educator and the narrative momentum of an accomplished journalist. Ideas unfold with measured depth, each paragraph offering both conceptual insight and practical resonance, ensuring the chapter functions as a definitive guide and an invitation to reflective engagement.

Ultimately, holding what matters demands mindfulness—a recognition that wealth, like time or knowledge, is finite and warrants careful stewardship. Such mindfulness fosters dignity, resisting the compulsive pursuit of ephemeral gains in favour of the quiet strength of permanence. It approaches uncertainty not with fear, but with preparedness, crafting a financial narrative that honours complexity while embracing responsibility. While this approach cannot eliminate volatility or loss, it provides a framework in which such challenges can be met with resilience and composure.

This chapter closes not with an endpoint, but by opening a space for ongoing engagement with the principles of thoughtful wealth. It equips readers to view financial decisions as expressions of identity and vision, enabling action with foresight and integrity. Holding what matters, therefore, becomes a lifelong practice—an active negotiation between material reality and aspirational meaning.

In the final analysis, the true value of gold and silver lies not in market quotations alone, but in their ability to anchor us amidst uncertainty, to provide clarity amidst complexity, and to affirm the dignity inherent in conscientious stewardship. This concluding reflection invites readers to carry forward these insights, re-entering their financial lives fortified by understanding, enriched by perspective, and committed to preserving what endures.

The final chapter offers a philosophical closure

The act of holding gold and silver transcends mere financial calculation; it is a profound statement about how we approach uncertainty, security, and legacy. As we reach this culminating point, the lens through which precious metals have been examined thus far sharpens into a philosophical clarity: these metals are not simply assets to be bought and sold but instruments of preparation, resilience, and mindful wealth. This chapter invites readers to re-enter their financial lives with a renewed sense of purpose—one grounded in permanence and dignity rather than transience and impulsivity. The implications of this shift ripple far beyond balance sheets, touching on the very way we understand value, control, and continuity in a world defined by change.

The volatile currents of contemporary finance, with their rapid innovation and opaque complexities, have distanced many from the tangible and enduring. Paper wealth can dissolve overnight; digital transactions, while convenient, often lack the reassurance of physical presence. Gold and silver reclaim this lost tangibility, anchoring wealth in matter that has weathered centuries and civilisations. This *physicality* offers more than security; it offers *agency*. To hold metal is to hold a tangible hedge against the unpredictable tides of policy, inflation, and geopolitical upheaval. Such agency, however, demands more than possession—it demands a *philosophy* of stewardship, an intentional mindset that perceives wealth as a dynamic interplay between preservation and purpose.

At its core, mindful wealth embraces a long view that honours permanence without succumbing to rigidity. Gold and silver are not inert hoards but living parts of a strategy designed to withstand the erosion of value and the fracturing of systems. They embody *resilience*, the capacity not only to survive shocks but to maintain options and flexibility in their aftermath. This resilience is inseparable from clarity—clarity about why one holds metals, what risks are being hedged, and how these assets fit within a broader tapestry of financial and personal priorities. Such clarity enables decisions that are measured, principled, and aligned with individual values rather than reactive impulses driven by fear or speculation.

The stories embedded within these metals—of survival, of foresight, of legacy—infuse them with meaning beyond market quotes. They represent a covenant between past and future, a tangible link that allows wealth to be a *vehicle for continuity*. This continuity challenges modern tendencies towards consumption and instant gratification, urging instead a perspective of wealth as *enduring capacity*. What is preserved through metals is not merely monetary worth but the *freedom to act*—to move, to protect, to support loved ones, and to contribute to causes larger than oneself. This emphasis on capacity redefines success, framing it as a matter of sustainable agency rather than transient luxury.

Real-world applications underscore the depth of this philosophy. Consider the individual who chooses physical bullion over purely digital exposure, not because it guarantees returns, but because it safeguards autonomy when systems falter. Or the family that designs a diversified storage plan, blending accessibility with concealment, thus securing wealth that can outlast turmoil and pass intact to future generations. These examples demonstrate that mindful wealth is neither passive nor simplistic; it is an active commitment to *intentional preparation*, demanding ongoing education, adaptability, and ethical reflection.

This chapter also confronts tensions inherent in holding precious metals. The balance between liquidity and permanence, visibility and privacy, immediacy and patience reflects broader questions about how we negotiate trust and control in modern financial landscapes. A mindful approach does not claim infallibility but advocates for humility—a recognition of uncertainty paired with deliberate actions that maximise stability without sacrificing opportunity. This stance challenges dominant narratives of wealth accumulation, replacing them with a framework where *stewardship* and *resilience* are paramount.

Throughout, the prose maintains an authoritative yet accessible tone, blending academic rigor with the clarity of a master teacher and the narrative allure of a skilled essayist. Each paragraph advances the reader's insight, unpacking complex ideas without sacrificing readability or engagement. The result is a chapter that not only synthesises preceding analysis but elevates it, positioning the reader to make decisions informed by both reason and reflection.

Ultimately, to hold gold and silver with clarity, permanence, and dignity is to affirm a profound human aspiration: to navigate an uncertain world with a steady hand and a considered heart. It is to acknowledge that wealth is not an end in itself but a *means to resilience*, a bulwark against chaos, and a legacy of intentionality. This concluding reflection offers not merely an endpoint but a launchpad—a foundation from which readers can approach their financial lives with renewed confidence and a deeper understanding of what it truly means to *hold what matters*.

About the Author

Calen Hart writes at the intersection of finance, philosophy, and personal sovereignty. With over a decade immersed in the dynamics of global markets, economic history, and human behavior, his work is driven by a single, evolving question: what does it mean to preserve value in an impermanent world? Hart's voice is both analytical and grounded, offering readers not just strategies, but clarity—an uncommon calm in the noise of modern finance. He believes real wealth begins with what you can hold, understand, and trust. Start Investing in Gold & Silver is his invitation to think deeper, act wiser, and build a legacy that lasts.

www.ingramcontent.com/pod-product-compliance
Lightning Source LLC
Chambersburg PA
CBHW031349230926
51848CB00002B/457
* 9 7 8 9 3 7 1 7 7 3 5 8 4 *